# The Many Paths of Christianity

Jan and Mel Thompson

Hodder & Stoughton

LONDON SYDNEY AUCKLAND TORONTO

Illustrated by Robina Green

**British Library Cataloguing in Publication Data**

Thompson, Jan
  The many paths of Christianity.
  1. Christian Church
  I. Title  II. Thompson, M. R. (Melvyn Rodney), 1946–
  260

  ISBN 0 7131 7767 5

First published 1988
Third impression 1989

© 1988 Jan and Mel Thompson

Printed in Great Britain for the educational publishing
division of Hodder and Stoughton Ltd, Mill Road, Dunton
Green, Sevenoaks, Kent by BPCC Wheatons Ltd, Exeter.

## Acknowledgements

The Publishers would like to thank the following for their
kind permission to include copyright material:

British Telecom for the extract from the Yellow Pages, p. 7;
Penguin Books for 'Pashka' from *The Food and Cooking* of
*Russia* by Lesley Chamberlain (Penguin Books 1983,
1988), © Lesley Chamberlain, p. 28; Richard Wells for
permission to use the front cover of an evangelical leaflet,
p. 75; The Seventh Day Adventist Church for the use of
their logo p. 80.

The Publishers would like to thank the following for
their kind permission to reproduce photographic material:

Christina Gasgoigne p. 12; Novosti p. 14; The Mansell
Collection Limited pp. 15, 38, 58, 60 top; John Twinning
pp. 16, 17 (both), 21, 23 (both), 24, 25 (both), 27 (both),
29, 46, 48, 50, 74; Barbara Heller Archive (courtesy of
Yanni Petsopoulos) p. 20; Topham Picture Library p. 26;
Popperfoto pp. 31, 43 (top), 56, 86 (bottom); Associated
Press Ltd p. 32; Carlos Reyes pp. 33, 42 (top), 45 (both),
49; Barnaby's Picture Library p. 34 (top left) Mervyn Rees,
p. 43 (bottom) G.A. Duncan; Caisse Nationale des
Monuments Historiques et des Sites p. 34 (top right);
Catholic Pictorial p. 34 (bottom left); H.W. Gates p34
(bottom right); Keith Ellis p. 37, 65, 69; Gwent College of
F.E. p. 40; Donna Thynne p. 41, 60 (bottom); Eddie Parker
p. 42 (bottom); R.L. Hudson p. 53, 67; Click/Chicago/Carol
Lee, Boston p. 57; The Salvation Army pp. 59, 62; British
Museum p. 60; Daisy Hayes p. 64; Camera Press pp. 66
Colin Davey; Clifford Shirley p. 71; J & M Thompson
pp. 72, 75 (right); Kingdom Faith Resource Centre p. 75;
The Church of Jesus Christ of Latter Day Saints pp. 77 &
78; Ray Dabrowski p. 80; Seventh Day Adventist Church
p. 80 (insert); Christian Science Committee on Publishing
p. 83; World Council of Churches p. 85, 87; Christian Aid
p. 86 (top).

**To Raymond, Carol, Katharine and Howard**

# Contents

# Preface

How often have you heard pupils refer to Christians and Catholics as though they belonged to two different religions? Have they asked you about Mormons or Jehovah's Witnesses? How many of us in Britain know much about Eastern Orthodoxy – a major branch of the Christian Church?

The recognition of different denominations should form an important part of the study of Christianity. Otherwise our pupils cannot begin to appreciate the rich diversity of this world religion. It is also a matter of general knowledge for those of us living in Christian countries. We should know why we are surrounded by so many different types of Churches. Some of these Churches may confront pupils through the media, in the High Street, or even on their doorstep. They should know what to expect.

This book has a general introduction to denominations, and concludes with a review of some alternative groups and the Ecumenical Movement. Otherwise, it is made up of three Parts: on the Orthodox, Roman Catholic and Protestant Churches. Each of these Parts is constructed in the same way, so that pupils can study one branch of the Church at a time, or thematically across the denominations.

Each Part finishes with a list of questions to test factual knowledge. There are also questions throughout to develop understanding and to give opportunities for imaginative and evaluative work. The Word List at the end explains most of the religious vocabulary in the book. Pupils should be encouraged to refer to this as often as necessary. There is also an index.

*The Many Paths of Christianity* is aimed at the lower and middle secondary school level. It could also be used by some GCSE pupils, since courses on Christianity require a general knowledge of the main divisions of the Christian Church, how the denominations came into existence, the common ground they share and their distinctive features. It could serve as an introduction to the syllabuses which require more detailed historical knowledge.

# Introduction
# Christian Denominations

If you look up 'Churches' in your Yellow Pages telephone directory, you will probably find a very long list. ('Church' should refer to the Christian people, but it is commonly used to describe the building where they meet.) Look closely, and you will find that there are different types of Churches: such as 'Assemblies of God', 'Baptist Church', 'Catholic Church', 'Elim Pentecostal Church' and 'Methodist Church'. Those which are simply listed as St Mary's, St Luke's, St Patrick's and so on, belong to the Church of England (also called the Anglican Church). They are all churches where Christians meet to worship God, but they belong to different denominations. The word *denomination* means 'name'. A new denomination is formed when a group of Christians call themselves by a new name, to show that in some way they are different from other Christians.

Christianity is a religion which can be practised in many different ways. Some Christians have elaborate forms of worship, with set prayers, statues and candles; others keep everything plain and simple. Some have priests, others do not. Some worship with excitement and dance, others in silence. Some accept great wealth, others choose poverty. Some take political action in the name of their religion; others think that Christianity is only to do with the individual and God, and should not be political at all. Some approve of war, if the cause is a just one; others think it is wrong to use violence under any circumstances (they are called pacifists).

These differences are a fact of religious life. This book will not try to argue that one form of Christianity is right and the others are wrong, or that one form is better or worse than another – although some

---

## 204   CHURCHES & CHURCH—CIVIL ENGINEERS

### Churches & church halls—contd.

Bible Way Tabernacle The,
    St. Barnabas Church Algernon Rd,SE13...01–691 3805
    Do.................................................01–692 0839
Brixton Unitarian Church, Effra Rd,CR0 .................01–655 0619
Bromley Christian Centre,
    Masons Hill,Bromley,BR2...01–460 1660
Bromley Common Methodist Church,
    Bloomfield Rd,BR2...01–460 7554
Catholic Churches (South London)—
    Cresswell Park, Blackheath,SE3.....................01–852 5420
    131 Deptford High St,Deptford,SE8.................01–692 2011
    Eltham High St,Eltham,SE9...........................01–850 1666
    5 Whitworth Rd,Norwood,SE25......................01–653 2806
Catholic Church of Our Lady of the Rosary,
    Brixton Rd,SW9...01–274 2367
Catholic Church St. Anselms, 89 West Hill.............Dartford 20075
Celestial Church of Christ—
    204a Coldharbour Lane,SW9.........................01–737 7927
Cherubim & Seraphim St. Michaels Church,
    65 Admaston Rd,SE18...01–854 3645
Christ Church, Lubbock Rd,Chislehurst,BR7.............01–467 1218
Christ Church, High St................................Swanley 65024
Christian Science—
    1st Church Bromley 54b Widmore Rd,BR1........01–460 2410
    8th Church London 20 Acre Lane,SW2.............01–274 3260
    10th Church London Meadowcourt Rd,SE3........01–852 2628
Church of God of Prophecy (Sydenham),
    Perry Rse.SE23...01–699 4708

St. Patricks Social Club, Hector St,Plumstead,SE18...01–854 0691
St. Saviours Catholic Church,
    175 Lewisham High St,SE13...01–852 2490
Salvation Army Corps & Community Centre—
    Gordon Rd,SE15....................................01–639 7292
Seventh Day Adventist Church, Selhurst Rd,SE25......01–653 7115
South East Hindu Association,
    (Temple) 5 Anglesea Avenue,SE18...01–854 4906
South London Mission—
    Peckham Methodist Ch Woods Rd,SE15...........01–639 8263
South Norwood Baptist Church,
    4 Oliver Avenue,SE25–01–653 5973
South Street Baptist Church,
    66 Greenwich S St,SE10...01–691 1270
St Paulinus Church Hall, Manor Rd ...................Crayford 522628
Stella Maris Church Hall, 66 Crooms Hill,SE10.........01–858 3968
Swanley Youth & Family Centre,
    Christ Church Kingswood Avenue...Swanley 62870
Swedish Seamen's Church, 120 Lower Rd,SE16 .........01–237 1644
    Do.................................................01–237 1956
Sydenham United Free Church, 2 Jews Walk,SE26...01–778 8601
Telford Canon Geo, Priests Ho Dockhead,SE1..........01–237 1641
Thamesmead Baptist Church, Titmuss Avenue,SE28...01–310 1683
Thamesmead Baptist Church,
    Yarnton Way,Erith,DA18...01–310 1816
Thamesmead Christian Community—
    St. Pauls Church Bentham Rd,SE28...............01–310 6814
    Church of the Cross Lensbury Way,SE2...........01–310 2419
Trinity Methodist Church Youth & Community Centre,
    Burrage Rd,SE18...01–317 7940

7

Christians will claim that their views are the only correct ones. Instead, we shall explore the rich variety of ways in which people have followed the Christian religion, seeing why one Church has divided off from another, and what each has to offer.

There are at least 1,000 million practising Christians in the world today. They are divided up into hundreds of denominations. These are some of the main ones:

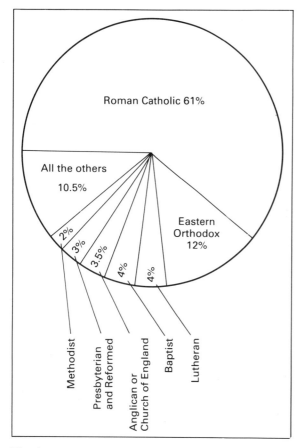

Fig. 1

The seven named here represent almost 90 per cent of all Christians. Most denominations are far too small to show on a diagram of this sort. In Africa, for example, there are many tiny Churches, some of which are found in only one place. They stay small because they quickly divide off from one another and adopt new names.

Most Christian denominations belong to three main branches of the Church:

1 The Eastern Orthodox Churches
2 The Roman Catholic Church
3 The Protestant Churches

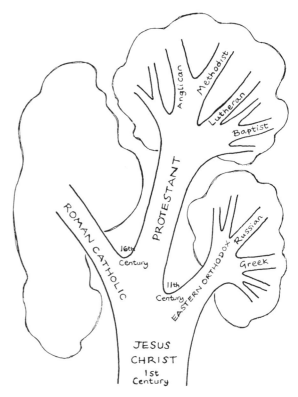

Fig. 2. Growth of the three main branches of Christianity

Notice on the diagram that the Roman Catholic and Eastern Orthodox Churches divided in the eleventh century. Then other Churches separated from the Catholic Church in the sixteenth century, at what is called the Reformation because they tried to *reform* the Church. These are called 'Protestant' because they grew out of a *protest* against the Roman Catholic Church.

Although claiming to be Christian, there are also groups which do not belong to these three main branches. The Jehovah's Witnesses and Christian Scientists, for example, have beliefs which are very different from those of other Christians.

**Map 1.** This map shows the branch to which the majority of Christians in each area belong today. Minority communities are not shown.

Orthodox

Catholic

Protestant

1 What was the original meaning of the word 'church', before it came to refer to a building? (Remember, you can look up important words in the Word List at the back of the book.)

2 (a) What does the word 'denomination' mean?
(b) Name one Christian denomination.
(c) Which is the nearest church to your school? To which denomination does it belong?
(d) Look up 'Churches' in the Yellow Pages. See how many different denominations you can find, and list them (just the denomination, not the name and address of each church).

3 Look at the paragraph beginning 'Christianity is a religion which can be practised in many different ways'.
(a) Do any of these descriptions appeal to you (e.g. silence; political action; pacifism)? Explain why.

(b) Take one pair of contrasts, and draw cartoon figures to show these particular differences between Christians.

4 (a) Using Fig. 1, name the largest of the Christian denominations.
(b) Still using Fig. 1, add up what percentage of the Christian community is Protestant. (Remember that the Church is divided into three main sections: Eastern Orthodox, Roman Catholic and Protestant.)
(c) Name a Christian group which does not belong to the three main branches of the Church.

9

# PART 1
# The Orthodox Churches

## WHERE, WHEN AND WHY

With more than 100 million members, the Orthodox Churches of the USSR, Eastern Europe and the Eastern Mediterranean continue a tradition of worship and belief that goes back to the earliest days of Christianity. The word *orthodox* means 'right belief'. It was first used to distinguish the majority of Christians from those who held different views. Later it became a title for the Eastern Churches which agreed together under the leadership of the Bishop of Constantinople.

The Orthodox Churches are named after the countries in which they are found. The map shows where the main ones are. All of these except the Greek Orthodox Church exist in Communist countries. The Coptic Church of Egypt separated from the rest of

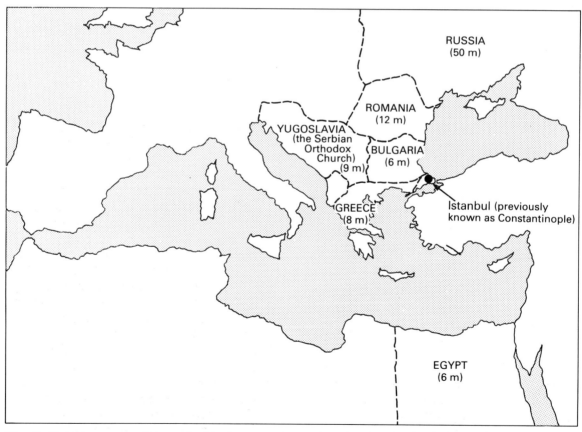

**Map 2.** Orthodox communities can be found throughout the world. They are called after the countries from which they come, e.g. you can find Russian, Greek and other Orthodox Churches in Britain. This map shows those countries in which the major Orthodox Churches originated.

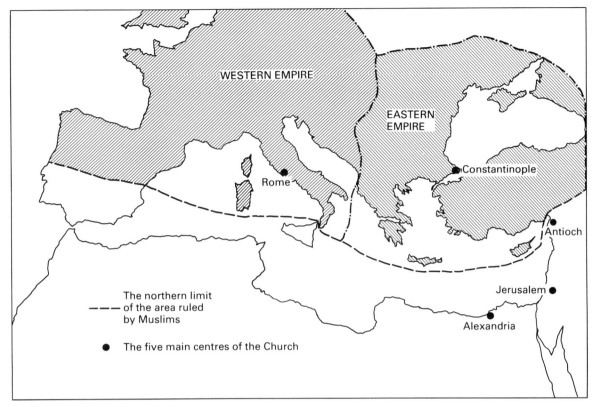

**Map 3.** 1054 CE — East and West divide

the Orthodox Churches in the sixth century.

The most senior leaders of these Churches are called patriarchs. On important matters of belief they come together under the leadership of the Patriarch of Constantinople, who is called the Ecumenical Patriarch (*patriarch* means 'great father' and *ecumenical* means 'of the whole world'). But each national church runs itself, and has its own special traditions and ceremonies.

Christianity started in the Mediterranean world of the first century, under the Roman Empire. During its first four hundred years, five main centres were established: **Rome** (the first capital of the Empire), **Constantinople** (the new capital built by Constantine, the first Christian emperor, in the fourth century), **Jerusalem** (where Christianity started), **Antioch** and **Alexandria**. Of these, Rome was in the western and the others in the eastern part of the Roman Empire.

In many ways the Empire was already divided between East and West. The East spoke Greek, the West spoke Latin, and there developed great rivalry between Rome and Constantinople. Then disaster struck Rome. In 410 it was attacked by Alaric the Visigoth and fell. The western part of the Empire was divided up by those whom the Romans called Barbarians. All that remained of the Roman Empire was in the east, ruled from Constantinople. In the seventh century the Arabs, united under the new religion of Islam, overran three of the eastern centres. This left only Constantinople.

Then on Christmas Day 800 the Bishop of Rome, Pope Leo III, revived the Western Empire by crowning Charlemagne as the new emperor. So once more there were two capital cities and two emperors. By the eleventh century, Rome and Constantinople – the old rivals – each with its own empire, confronted one another.

There were five points of disagreement between the Eastern Orthodox Churches and the Roman Catholic Church, as the two sides were called:

(i) Constantinople, as a capital of the Empire, would not accept second place to Rome. It demanded equality.

(ii) The pope (a title used for the Bishop of Rome) claimed to be supreme over all bishops, and to have ultimate authority in matters of belief. The Eastern bishops said that the pope was no more than first among equals, and that, on matters of faith, decisions must be taken by all the bishops together in councils.

(iii) Christians in the West had adopted a change in the wording of the Creed (the statement of their beliefs). This meant a different way of describing the relationship between Christ and the Holy Spirit. The East accused the West of false teaching, because it affected the central Christian idea about God the Trinity (Father, Son and Holy Spirit).

(iv) The East used ordinary bread for the Communion, but the West used flat, unleavened wafers.

(v) In the West, priests were not allowed to marry, but in the East married men became local priests.

Things came to a head in the year 1054. A representative of the pope went to Constantinople and there excommunicated the patriarch (that is, he declared him to be outside the true Church). The patriarch retaliated in a similar way against the pope.

In 1453, Constantinople was attacked by the Turks. The emperor was killed in the

In the fourth century the Emperor Constantine built a new capital city for the Roman Empire. He named it Constantinople, after himself. When the Muslims took the city in the fifteenth century they renamed it Istanbul. The skyline today is dominated by Muslim mosques.

fighting and the city fell. Although under Turkish rule, the patriarch was allowed to continue his religious authority. He was given the emperor's crown as a sign of this. For much of their history, the Eastern Orthodox Churches have existed under political authority. First it was the Romans, then the Muslims and Turks and (in recent times) the Communist regimes of Eastern Europe.

1 Match up these four words with their correct meanings:

orthodox
patriarch
creed
excommunication

great father
cut off from the Church
right belief
statement of belief

2 Using Map 2:
(a) Name the largest Eastern Orthodox Church.
(b) Name a Communist country where there are Orthodox Christians.
(c) What is the modern name of the city in Turkey where the Ecumenical Patriarch lives now?

3 Using Map 3:
(a) Name the four eastern centres of the Church in the Roman Empire.
(b) Which of these became the most important?

4 Make a time chart of all the dates and events mentioned in this chapter, from the paragraph beginning 'Christianity started in the Mediterranean world. . .'

5 Five issues which divided the Orthodox and Catholic Churches are listed (p. 12).
(a) Which of these do you think was the most important when the Churches first divided?
(b) Should this still be an important issue today?

# BUILDINGS

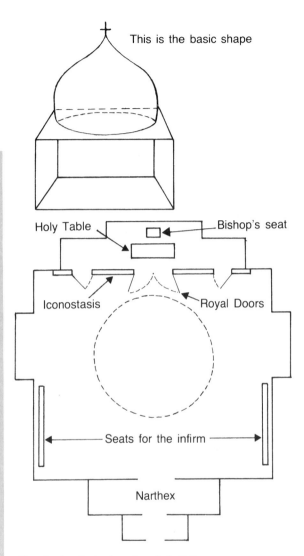

**Fig. 3.** An Orthodox church building

Orthodox church buildings are basically square in shape, topped by a circle – a dome. The design of the church building expresses the Orthodox Christian view of the world. The square is thought to represent correctness, organisation and equality (it has four equal sides and four right angles). Standing within the square, people feel called together and equal before

13

Kiev Cathedral, USSR. Many Orthodox churches, like this one, make the basic shape more elaborate. You can still see that it is square (this is emphasised here by the turrets in each corner) and has a circular dome. The onion-shaped domes are typical of Russian Orthodox church buildings.

As you go into an Orthodox Church, you pass through a large entrance hall, called the narthex. This represents the stage when someone wants to become a Christian. The main worship area represents the whole body of the Church. In their lives, Orthodox Christians think of themselves as being encouraged and helped not just by their fellow Christians alive in the present, but also by those of the past who have died. As the present generation of Christians stands on the floor of the church, they are surrounded on the walls by images of holy Christians (the saints) who have lived before them. These images naturally lead upwards to the ceiling, where Christ is seated in the most important place, high up in the centre.

Right across the front of the church there is a screen called an *iconostasis*. On it are pictures of the four Gospel writers and scenes from the life of Christ. In the iconostasis there are three doors. One leads to the vestry where the priests dress for the services and where the book for the Gospel readings is kept. Another leads to an area called the Chapel of the Preparation. This is where the bread and wine are prepared for the Liturgy, the most important service (known by some other Churches as Holy Communion). The third is a double door at the very centre of the iconostasis. Behind this is the Holy Table on which the bread and wine are made holy as the Body and Blood of Christ. These central doors are called the Royal Doors, and are opened at the climax of the Liturgy.

The holiest parts of the Liturgy are regarded as a mystery which should not be watched directly by the people, who are separated from it by the screen. This expresses the idea that a person cannot see God directly, but only through those things in which God chooses to reveal himself. Therefore, when the worshipper looks straight ahead towards the most holy place, he or she is presented with images of the life of Christ. The opening of the Royal Doors is a celebration of Christ coming to the people, breaking through the barrier

God. The floor represents Earth, where the people are gathered. The four corners represent the four Gospel writers (Matthew, Mark, Luke and John). As your eye is led upwards, the richly decorated ceiling represents heaven. The circle of the dome expresses the eternity of God – since it has no beginning or end, and on the top of it there stands a cross.

A twelfth-century mosaic on the inside of the dome of an Orthodox church building

(a) The central image, as here, is always of Jesus Christ (represented by the Greek letters IC XC). In the dome, he is always shown as Pantocrator — meaning 'Ruler of all'. Can you find the Greek word ΠΑΝΤΟΚΡΑΤWP?

(b) Why do you think the picture of Jesus takes pride of place?

(c) How would you describe Jesus in this picture?

which naturally separates them from God.

In traditional Orthodox churches there are no seats, except a few around the walls for the old and weak. People stand for prayer, usually with men on one side of the church building and women on the other. Sometimes they may move about the church during the Liturgy, going to pray before an icon (a special holy picture) and silently greeting other people that they know.

1 Draw a plan or a sketch of the interior of an Orthodox church building. Label those things which have special meaning and, in a key, note down what each of them represents.
2 Copy out the definition of the word 'mystery' from the Word List at the back of this book.

# PRIESTS AND MINISTERS

From New Testament times, there have been special people appointed to lead and organise the churches. These can generally be called ministers, because they minister to the needs of the people, or help and serve them. The Orthodox Churches continue the tradition of having only men to do this, who may become bishops, priests or deacons.

The word *deacon* means 'servant' or 'minister'. The deacon's role is to assist the priest and represent the people. During services he stands in front of the iconostasis (while the priest is behind it at the Holy Table) and leads the congregation.

The most important service in the Church

An iconostasis

(a) Look up 'icon' in the Word List, and then say how many icons there are in this photograph.
(b) Why do you think the special doors in the centre are called the Royal Doors?
(c) When would you find the Royal Doors open?

(the Liturgy), when bread and wine is made holy as the Body and Blood of Christ, can only be led by priests and bishops. A man should normally be at least thirty before he can become a priest. He will have to decide whether or not he wishes to be married beforehand. Those who marry can work in the local churches, but they will never be able to become bishops. These ordinary parish priests have a life that is similar to that of their people. Their training is not as long as for those who remain unmarried and who may go on to take up senior posts in the Church. A man may not marry after he

Fig. 4. An Orthodox bishop

Answer after reading this section:
(a) Copy the symbol on the top of his crook into your book, and explain its significance.
(b) Whose image is on the enkolpion? Explain why.

has been ordained a priest, and if his wife dies he is not allowed to marry again.

The most important role is that of a bishop, who is in charge of a number of churches. Bishops and priests of the Orthodox Churches generally have beards. Priests usually wear black cassocks and may also have round black hats. For special ceremonies, bishops wear elaborate clothes (called vestments). They may wear headdresses in the shape of crowns, topped with a cross and with pictures on the sides. These come from a tradition that the bishops have taken over the authority of the old emperors of the Eastern Roman Empire. Notice (in Fig. 4) that the bishop is carrying a shepherd's crook. This proclaims that he is to be a shepherd of his people. On top of the crook there is a symbol for Christ. It contains a circle, within which the

Answer after reading this section:
(a) How can you tell that this is an Orthodox bishop, although he is not wearing ceremonial costume?
(b) What features are common to both priests and bishops?

17

Greek letters *Chi* and *Rho* are worked together. These are the first letters of the Greek word *Christos*, meaning 'Christ'. On either side of these are the first and last letters of the Greek alphabet – *Alpha* and *Omega*, which come from a saying in the New Testament that Christ is the first and the last. The bishop also has a medallion round his neck (called an *enkolpion*). It usually has on it a picture of the Virgin Mary. In Orthodox thought, Mary often represents the whole of the Christian community.

Those who are chosen to become bishops must be monks. There are both monks and nuns in the Orthodox Churches. Monks live together under the rule of an abbot (called an *archimandrite*). Abbots are elected, and each monastery has its own rules. Some monks are ordained and may later become bishops or abbots; but many others are not priests, and simply choose the monastic life.

1 Place these in order of seniority, starting with the most important: priest, bishop, deacon.
2 Draw an Orthodox bishop either in ordinary or ceremonial dress and label all the things of special significance.
3 The special clothes worn by a bishop express what he stands for. What is there about your own appearance (e.g. clothes, badges, hairstyle) which shows your interests and attitudes?
4 Imagine that you are a man who is to become an Orthodox priest. You have not yet found a partner, but are thinking about marriage. List the advantages and disadvantages of marriage for your work in the Church. (You do not know whether or not you might ever become a bishop, so think mainly about your life as a parish priest, helping the people of your community.)
5 Is a comfortable life a hindrance to being religious? Can you think of any advantages of being a monk or a nun?

# PRAYER AND WORSHIP

Orthodox Christians often make the sign of the cross as a simple act of worship. They do it many times during the course of a day, such as when entering a church building, standing for a moment of prayer before an icon, as a grace before meals or when passing a wayside shrine.

**Fig. 5**

1. Forehead (mind)
2. Heart (emotions)
3. Right shoulder )
4. Left shoulder ) (strength)

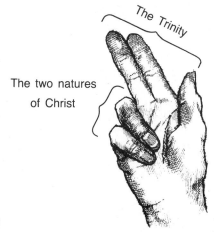

The Trinity

The two natures of Christ

**Fig. 6**

With the right hand, they touch first the forehead (representing the mind), then the heart (the person's feelings and innermost self) and finally the right and left shoulders (their strength). It is an act of offering all of their life to Christ. The first two fingers and thumb are joined together – as a reminder of the three persons of the Holy Trinity: God the *Father*, *Son* and *Holy Spirit*. The word *trinity* means 'three-in-one', and it is an important Christian belief that God is known in these three ways. The other two fingers are folded back into the palm of the hand. They stand for the belief in the two natures of Jesus Christ – that he was both fully *human* and yet also *God*. While making the sign, the person says 'In the name of the Father, and of the Son, and of the Holy Spirit.'

The same two religious ideas – the Trinity and the two natures of Christ – are proclaimed when a priest or bishop blesses the people. He may hold in his hands two candlesticks: the *trikirion* with three candles, and the *dikirion* with two.

![Fig. 7]()

**Fig. 7.** A blessing with the dikirion and trikirion

Which represents the Trinity? What does the other represent?

Another simple act of private worship widely used in the Orthodox Churches is the Jesus Prayer. This consists of repeating these words: 'Jesus Christ, Son of God, have mercy upon me, a sinner.' It can be said over and over again, while the person reflects on the meaning of the words. Some people try to say it in rhythm with their breathing, so that it becomes almost an unconscious act of praying while they go about their ordinary work.

Inside an Orthodox Church are many wall paintings and icons (special holy pictures) of Jesus or the saints. You are bound to see an icon of the Virgin Mary, the most important saint, who is normally called 'Mother of God' because she gave birth to Jesus.

These paintings are not for decoration, but are used to help people when they pray. Candles may be burned in front of icons, and the icons can be kissed and carried in procession. Such devotion to an icon enables a worshipper to think about the person represented on it. They are also a means of teaching – by showing scenes from the life of Christ, for example.

How can you tell that this picture of St Andrew is an icon and not an ordinary painting?

In the early days of the Church there was a debate about images. Some welcomed them as aids to worship, while others feared that they might be worshipped for themselves, which would be idolatry. The Orthodox Churches decided that images could be given veneration (held in great respect as holy objects) but not true worship.

Orthodox Christians think of the saints as present with them, and may ask them for advice or help. Often they express this by lighting a candle in front of an image of the saint. Anniversaries of saints are celebrated with feasting and with the saint's icon being carried in procession. When a person is named after a saint (which is usual among Orthodox), that saint's day is treated like a second birthday. It is called the person's 'Name Day'.

Orthodox worship is very colourful. Candles flicker before icons, and there is incense and music. All this adds to the sense of awe and holiness. During the Liturgy (when bread and wine is given to the people to eat as the Body and Blood of Christ), incense is waved over the Holy Table and before the priests, the icons and the people. Unlike most other denominations, the Orthodox Churches do not use musical instruments in their worship (although they do have bells). Singing is always unaccompanied. They think that this is a more pure and natural form of music.

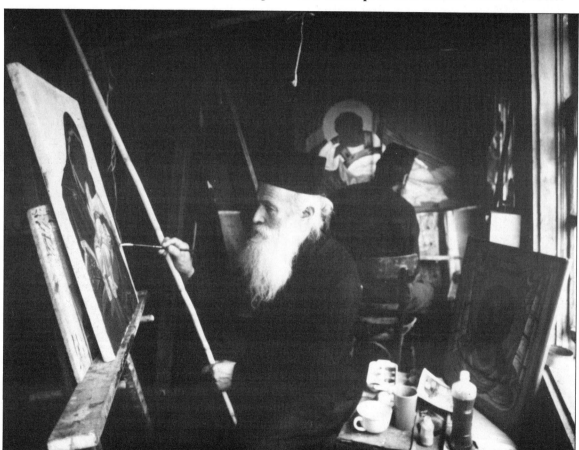

Painting an icon is seen as an important religious task, and is often done by monks. Prayers are said before the work begins; and the icon is blessed with holy water before being used in worship.

The icon painter does not sign his work — for he sees himself as a servant of the Church, not using his own imagination, but producing a traditional image.

1 When Christians speak of God as the Holy Trinity, of which three 'persons' are they thinking?
2 What are the differences in the way an icon and an ordinary painting are done?
3 Explain in your own words the difference between venerating an icon, and actually worshipping it, which would be idolatry.
4 There are five senses – sight, hearing, touch, taste and smell. How are each of these used in the course of Orthodox worship?
5 (a) Write out the Jesus Prayer as attractively as you can.
   (b) Choose one word or phrase from it and try to find out what it could mean to a Christian.

# THE LITURGY

In the Orthodox Churches the most important act of worship is called the Liturgy. Although other Churches use different names for it, such as Holy Communion or the Eucharist, the main parts of this service are common to most Christian denominations. There are prayers, and readings from the Bible to prepare the people. Then bread and wine are taken to the Holy Table to be consecrated (made holy) by the priest before being shared out among the people. This service repeats what Jesus did among his disciples at the Last Supper, the night before his death.

During supper Jesus took bread, and having said the blessing he broke it and

At the climax of the Liturgy the Royal Doors of the iconostasis are thrown open and the priest comes out with what is believed to be the Body and Blood of Christ, to give to the people. Bread and wine are given together on a spoon directly into the mouth.

People line up and walk forward to receive it standing. This photograph shows a young child being held up for the bread and wine. As the people leave, they take the antidoron from the plate in the foreground.

21

gave it to the disciples with the words: 'Take this and eat; this is my body.' Then he took a cup, and having offered thanks to God he gave it to them with the words: 'Drink from it, all of you. For this is my blood, the blood of the covenant, shed for many for the forgiveness of sins.' (Matthew 26:26–8)

Orthodox Christians believe that God the Holy Spirit comes upon the bread and wine, making it into the Body and Blood of Christ. It still looks like bread and wine, but it now makes Christ present to believers in a special way. This is regarded as a great mystery, which people will never fully understand, however old they are. So even small children are allowed to receive the Body and Blood of Christ. From the age of about seven years, however, they must prepare themselves for it in the same way as an adult, by making a private confession of their sins to a priest.

The bread used in the service is either baked by the monks or brought by the people. That which is taken to the Holy Table is called *prosphora*. The rest is distributed at the end of the service and people can take it home with them. It is called the *antidoron*, and represents the earliest tradition of the Church when people would meet to share a full meal together. Some people regard taking the consecrated bread and wine as such an important thing that they only receive it on major festivals and after serious preparation. The antidoron is their way of sharing in the Liturgy on the other occasions.

Much of the service takes place behind the closed doors of the iconostasis, showing that it is a mystery that is only partly to be seen. Yet, despite this sense of mystery, each Orthodox Church (Greek, Russian etc.) celebrates the Liturgy, and the priest preaches the Christian Gospel, in the ordinary language of the people.

The Liturgy is one of seven Mysteries in the Orthodox tradition (called sacraments in some other Churches). These are things which are believed to bring about spiritual benefit. The others are: Baptism and Confirmation, Penance (the confession required before sharing fully in the Liturgy), Anointing of the sick, Marriage and Orders (the service in which a man is made a priest).

1 Draw bread and wine and explain beneath them what they represent for Orthodox Christians when they have been consecrated in the Liturgy.
2 What was the origin of this service?
3 What names do other Churches call this service?
4 Why do some people only take the antidoron, rather than the consecrated bread and wine?
5 Why do you think seven is chosen as the age from which children must prepare themselves fully before receiving the Body and Blood of Christ?
6 Much of the Liturgy takes place behind closed doors.
(a) Why do you think some people value the sense of the hidden and the mysterious in religion?
(b) Can you think of anything else (not necessarily to do with religion) which is fascinating because it is mysterious or partly hidden?
(c) What is the special excitement about sharing a secret?

# STAGES IN LIFE

**Baptism**
The Orthodox Churches baptise babies. The priest plunges the naked child three times into a font (a large basin of water), in the name of the Father, the Son and the Holy Spirit. In the Orthodox Churches, unlike some Western denominations, the child actually goes into the water rather than just being sprinkled with it. Baptism represents both the washing away of sins, and being born again as a child of God.

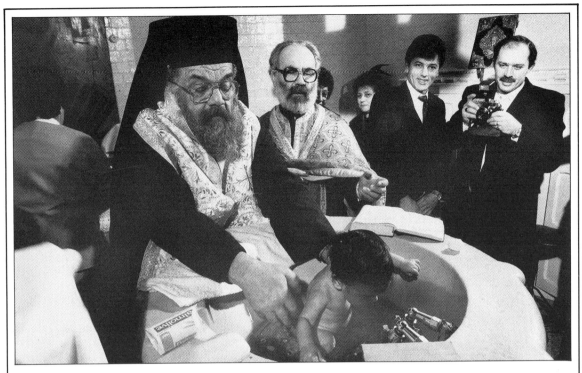

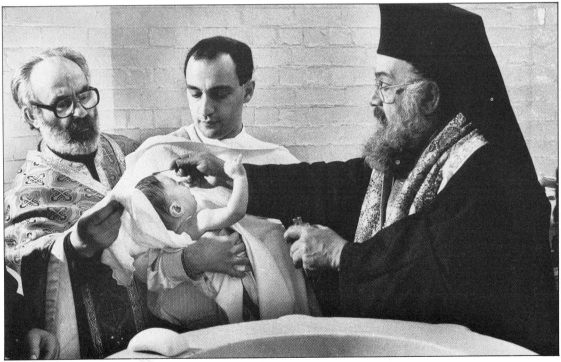

After reading the section on baptism, write your own captions to these two photographs.

The child is then dressed in white, and is anointed with oil by the priest. With the oil, he makes the sign of the cross on the child's forehead, then on the eyelids, nostrils, ears, lips, chest, hands and feet. As he does so he says 'the seal of the gift of the Holy Spirit'. This ceremony is called Chrismation, and is the equivalent of the Confirmation service that in other Churches would be left until the child is old enough to answer for himself or herself. Ointment is used for healing, and symbolises the hope that the child will grow strong in the Christian faith, with the help of God's Holy Spirit.

A small lock of hair is clipped off. This is an old religious custom to show that the child is now to be committed to the Christian religion. The child is also given a cross to wear round its neck for the rest of its life.

Once baptised and anointed in this way, the child is a full member of the Church, and can receive the consecrated bread and wine.

## Marriage

The marriage service in the Orthodox Churches has some things in common with Western marriages. Rings are exchanged and the couple have to declare that they are free and willing to marry. There are also special customs which express the meaning of marriage.

The bride and groom also kiss an icon, which is then to become the special icon they will keep in their home.

In some countries, only civil marriage is legal. A couple may therefore have to go to a registry office for a civil marriage and then to the church to have the marriage blessed. Bishops have the authority to grant divorce, and the church will then bless the next marriage.

In the Russian Orthodox Church, the marriage service is called 'Crowning' and the couple have silver or golden crowns put on their heads in the service. The one which the man receives has the image of Christ on it, and the woman's has that of the Virgin Mary. The crowns are signs of the dignity and importance of marriage. The Greek Orthodox Church has a similar ceremony, using garlands, as in these photographs.

(a) The bride and groom share a cup of wine together. What do you think this stands for?

(b) The priest leads them round in a circle. A circle has no end, so what do you think this is meant to show about the meaning of marriage?

## Death

Open coffin at a Russian Orthodox funeral

1. What is the significance of being buried in the waters of baptism and coming up again?
2. Draw a picture of a baby and indicate the parts of the body which are sealed with oil at Chrismation.
3. Oil is used at Chrismation, and also to anoint the sick.
   (a) Why is oil used as a symbol of healing?
   (b) Name an ointment which is used today to heal sores and wounds.
4. Look up I Corinthians 15:35-7.
   (a) Explain in your own words what the corn symbolises.
   (b) Why then is a dish of corn set out in the church?
5. (a) What do lighted candles mean to you? Write down the first idea that comes into your mind.
   (b) Candles are lit at funerals. Why do you think they are used as symbols of life?
   (c) Read John 8:12. What do you think Jesus meant when he spoke of himself as the Light of the World?

Whenever possible, a person who has died is brought into the church building and is laid out in an open coffin, surrounded by flowers. The lid of the coffin is left open so that the mourners can see the body and pay their last respects. A strip of cloth is sometimes put over the forehead of the body (as in this photograph). On it are images of Jesus, Mary, and John the Baptist. Like the victory wreath of an athlete, it expresses the idea that the person has completed his or her earthly race.

During the funeral service, mourners hold lighted candles. These represent Christ as the Light of the World and as the giver of new life. Sometimes one part of the church building is set aside for prayers for those who have died. People light candles there, and there may be a dish of corn set out (see question 4).

# FESTIVALS

The most important festival for the Orthodox Churches is Easter (called Pascha). During the previous week there is a series of events leading up to this. Here is a brief description of some of the many ceremonies found in Orthodox Churches during this week.

## Palm Sunday

On the Sunday before Easter, branches are brought into the church. This is a reminder of when Jesus rode into Jerusalem, and crowds cut down palm branches to put on the road in front of him as a gesture of welcome and respect.

Crosses made of dried palm leaves are set out for members of the congregation to take.

Great Friday

## Great Thursday

At the Last Supper, Jesus washed the feet of his disciples. During this evening the bishop will wash the feet of some of his priests, following the action of Jesus, as a sign of humility and service. A bishop will also bless the oils which are given out to his priests, for use in anointing the newly baptised children during the coming year.

## Great Friday

A cloth with an image of Jesus on it is brought out and arranged on a stand in the middle of the church. This is like the laying out of a dead body because this recalls the Friday when Jesus died. People stand round it holding candles, like mourners. They may also go forward to kiss the image of Christ on the cloth.

## Great Saturday

There may be a funeral procession round the church, with the cloth being carried ahead of the mourners. Tradition sees this day after the crucifixion as a time when Jesus went to preach to those who were dead. Prayers are therefore said for those who have died.

This is also the day for bringing into the church the special food which will be eaten the next day. Often there are coloured eggs, some decorated very elaborately. (People crack these eggs together, rather like the tradition of pulling Christmas crackers. It is a sign of the breaking open of Christ's tomb at Easter.) In the Russian Church there are pyramid-shaped cheesecakes, and pastries made with spices and raisins. The foods are set out on tables to be blessed, with candles set among them.

# Special treat for Russian Easter: Pashka

Pashka is a mixture of tvorog (curd cheese) with nuts, dried fruits and sugar, enriched with cream, eggs and butter.

There are many different ways to make Pashka: it can be made as a blend of the raw ingredients which are then kept in a mould for 24 hours, or baked in an oven, or made from cooked curd cheese, while the rest of the ingredients are raw.

The recipe for an uncooked Pashka is:

$1\frac{1}{4}$ lb (600 g) curd cheese
1 oz (30 g) unsalted butter
3 tablespoons double cream
3 medium size eggs
$\frac{1}{4}$ lb (110 g) caster sugar

$\frac{1}{4}$ lb (110 g) almonds
$\frac{1}{4}$ lb (110 g) raisins or candied peel, or a mixture of them
$\frac{1}{2}$ teaspoon vanilla essence

Beat the butter with a wooden spoon to soften it. Add it to the curd cheese and mix it thoroughly. Separate the eggs, placing the whites in a clean bowl, any trace of grease will prevent the egg whites from whipping successfully.

Whisk the egg yolks together with the caster sugar, until the mixture is thick and rather pale in colour. Add the egg yolks and sugar to the curd cheese. Sprinkle in the vanilla essence and beat all together to remove any lumps.

Whip the egg whites till they form stiff peaks. Separately whip the cream and gently fold it into the curd cheese mixture using a tablespoon. Chop the almonds and mix them with the curd cheese, together with the raisins.

Now the Pashka should be poured into a mould and left under a weight for 24 hours to drain the excess liquid. My grandmother had a beautiful pyramid-shaped mould (those made from palm wood were the best, I heard) with the imprint of flowers, birds and different geometrical ornaments. When the Pashka was turned out the imprint was left on the surface of the cheese. Nowadays a clay or plastic flower-pot can be a substitute.

Line the mould with muslin, letting it overhang for several inches to fold over the top. Spoon in the Pashka mixture. Fold the ends of the muslin over the top and cover with a little plate or saucer, which is smaller in size than the wide top of the pot. Weigh it down with a two pound weight or a milk bottle filled with water. Rest the pot on a plate to collect any liquid, which will come down through the hole. Put the pot with Pashka in a refrigerator for 24 hours.

Shake out the Pashka on to a serving plate and decorate with nuts or raisins.

(By Valya Ivanova, in Lesley Chamberlain, *The Food and Cooking of Russia*.)

As midnight approaches, the cloth is removed from the church, which stands dark and empty, like Christ's tomb. The people walk round the outside of the church with candles. The doors of the church are closed (like the entrance to the tomb) and the people, led by a priest carrying an icon and a cross, stand outside.

### Pascha (Easter Sunday)

At midnight, the doors are flung open and the priest announces 'Christ is risen!' The people reply 'He is risen indeed!' Light floods into the church. People stand holding their candles as the Liturgy starts, bells are rung, and in Greece there are sirens and fireworks as well.

At midnight at this Orthodox church, a special bell is rung outside the church.

During the whole of the week after Easter, a large loaf rests on the Holy Table. Called the *artos* (the Greek word for bread), it has an image representing Christ pressed into the top of it. It is there to express the theme of Jesus as the Bread of Life.

The early Church decided that Easter should be celebrated on the first Sunday following the full moon on or after the spring equinox. That meant that it could fall on any Sunday between 22 March and 25 April. A problem arose, however, for the Eastern Church continued to use the Julian calendar when the Western Church changed to the Gregorian calendar in the sixteenth century. The result is that the Orthodox and Western Churches celebrate Easter on different days most years – although from time to time the two calendars agree.

Many of the Orthodox festivals are the same as those in the West, and we shall look at them later (e.g. Christmas). Some have special ceremonies attached to them in the Orthodox Churches. For example, 6 January is called Epiphany in the West and it celebrates the arrival of the Wise Men to see the infant Jesus; but the East has kept the older association with Jesus' baptism. At one time this was one of the days specially set aside for baptisms, and on the day before that feast it is still customary to bless the waters. In an open-air ceremony – in freezing conditions in the Russian winter – water in a font is blessed. The people take jars of water home to sprinkle round the house as an act of blessing. There are prayers that the water may cleanse and protect from evil, and a cross is dipped into it three times.

As well as these times of celebration and feasting, Orthodox Christians practise fasting. People have different ways of keeping a fast. Some limit what they eat, and others use it as a time to do without some other luxuries. The idea is not punishment, but to gain self-discipline. The longest period of fasting is the forty days before Easter, called Lent. Every week,

Friday is observed as the day of the crucifixion, and Wednesday as the day when Jesus was betrayed by Judas. Some Orthodox Christians fast on these days. During a fast, icons may be draped in black, and the priests wear only black vestments.

By contrast, each week, Sunday is celebrated as the day of the Resurrection. The Russian word for Sunday is *Voskresnie*, which means 'resurrection'.

1 Read Mark 11:1–10. Copy out the verse that best illustrates Palm Sunday.
2 Read John 13:1–5 and 12–17.
(a) Explain in your own words *why* Jesus washed his disciples' feet.
(b) Why is this practice continued in the Church today?
3 Remembering what happened on the Sunday after Jesus' death, why do you think the day of his crucifixion is now called Great Friday?
4 What two symbols represent Christ's tomb for Orthodox Christians?
5 Read John 6:33–5. Jesus is not talking here about bodily hunger and thirst, but about spiritual life. Write out verse 35 in your own words.
6 Draw a labelled diagram of the main events that lead up to the celebration of Easter in the Orthodox Churches.
7 The Orthodox Easter is like a drama, with the church as the stage and the people as actors. What are the advantages of acting out something which could just as well be explained by word of mouth or in writing?
8 Working as a group, choose one of the days connected with Easter, and act out what is done on that day in an Orthodox church.
9 (a) What does it mean to go on a fast?
(b) List all the reasons you can think of why someone might fast.
(c) Underline the religious reasons in the list you have just made.

# CHECK YOUR READING ON THE ORTHODOX CHURCHES

1 What does 'orthodox' mean?
2 Name one of the Orthodox Churches.
3 In which country are you most likely to find Coptic Christians?
4 What does 'patriarch' mean?
5 Which five cities had patriarchs in the early years of the Church?
6 Who is the main leader of the Orthodox Churches today?
7 What would you expect to see on the inside walls of an Orthodox church building?
8 Whose image would you see on the inside of the dome?
9 Whose image is usually on the bishop's medallion?
10 Which Orthodox priests may not marry?
11 How do the Orthodox cross themselves? themselves?
12 What is the 'Jesus Prayer'?
13 What is an icon?
14 How are icons treated?
15 What goes on behind the iconostasis?
16 What two things are consecrated as symbols for Christ in the Liturgy?
17 What can you take home with you from the Liturgy?
18 When is Chrismation done?
19 What is used in the Chrismation ceremony?
20 What are put on the heads of the bride and groom at a Russian Orthodox wedding?
21 What do people light at funerals?
22 What is celebrated on the Sunday before Easter?
23 When do the Easter Day celebrations start in Orthodox countries?
24 What event in Jesus' life is remembered by the Orthodox Churches on 6 January?
25 What does the Russian name for Sunday mean?

# PART 2
# The Roman Catholic Church

## WHERE, WHEN AND WHY

Catholics outnumber all other Christians, and can be found throughout the world (*catholic* means 'worldwide'). They are called *Roman* Catholics because they are led by the pope, the Bishop of Rome, believed to be the successor of St Peter the first bishop of Rome. Peter was the most important of the twelve disciples, called Apostles, and he became the first leader of the Church after Jesus' death. Because of his importance, and because Rome was the capital city of the Empire, the Church of Rome claimed to have a special position within the Christian community.

By the fifth century, the pope claimed to have authority over all other bishops. This was because, according to Matthew's Gospel, St Peter had been told by Jesus that

St Peter's, the largest church building in the world, is in Vatican City — the pope's official place of residence in Rome. In this photograph people crowd into St Peter's Square to receive the pope's blessing on Easter Day. According to tradition, St Peter founded the church in Rome and was put to death here in 64 CE when Nero was emperor. If so, he was probably buried beneath this church.

he was to be the rock on which the Church would be built; and the popes were St Peter's successors in Rome. This authority was disputed by the other patriarchs, or leaders, of the Church; and as the Empire was divided East from West, Rome came to control the western part of the Empire, separated from the Greek-speaking East.

The power of the popes grew. Pope Leo III crowned the Emperor Charlemagne in 800 – a sign that a political ruler should receive his authority from the Church. But with that power came increasing corruption, in spite of many attempts at reform. In the centuries before the Protestant Reformation (see pp. 55–6) people sometimes paid money to get positions of power in the Church. This was called 'simony' and led to some Church leaders living like princes and having little interest in the religious welfare of those they ruled. After the separation of the Protestant Churches in the sixteenth century, the Catholic Church itself had a period of reform, usually called 'The Counter Reformation'.

Traditionally, Catholics have spoken of the four marks of the Church:

**One**
There can be only one Church, founded by Christ himself and his Apostles. Groups of people may leave the Church or join it again, but the Church itself remains one.

**Holy**
To be holy is to be specially chosen and set apart for God's work. It is believed that God has established his Church and makes it holy, in spite of the human failings of those within it.

**Catholic**
This means 'worldwide', and was originally used of the whole Church before its divisions became permanent.

The title *pope* means 'father', and he is also referred to as the Holy Father. Although the pope is very important as the head of the Roman Catholic Church, he is also called *servus servorum dei* — Latin for 'Servant of the servants of God'. His task is to be first among his brother bishops in serving the Church.

This photograph shows Pope John Paul II in the Vatican Palace with cardinals soon after his election in 1978. The cardinals are important leaders of the Church who meet together in Rome when the pope dies to choose which of them should become the next pope.

The ordination of a Roman Catholic priest by the laying on of hands

## Apostolic

The Church was founded by the Apostles and it is believed that their authority has been handed down from one person to another in what is called the 'Apostolic Succession'. Every time a man is made a priest or bishop, this authority is passed on, expressed by a bishop laying his hands on his head.

Catholics today may describe the Church in many other ways. They emphasise, for instance, that it is a community of the people of God, among whom Christ's Spirit is at work.

Today many Catholics work alongside Christians of other denominations, but until recently they called the others 'separated brethren'. Since Catholics believe that the Church is one and apostolic, they cannot see the Catholic Church as just one option among others, but as the central Church from which the others have broken away. As with the Orthodox Churches of the East, the Catholic Church of Rome has its traditions going back to the earliest years of Christianity, and this is the source of its claim to authority. However, there is greater willingness today in the Catholic Church to recognise that there may be truth to be found in other Christian denominations.

1 Explain why the Bishop of Rome became so important.
2 Copy out Matthew 16:18.
3 Do you know the name of the present pope?
4 Draw a diagram to show what Catholics believe to be the four marks of the Church.
5 Why do Catholics sometimes call Christians of other denominations 'separated brethren'?
6 Define in your own words: (a) holy (b) apostolic (c) pope. (They are in the Word List at the back of the book.)

33

# BUILDINGS

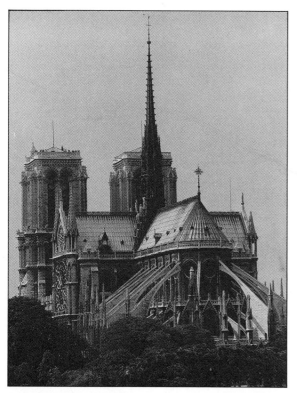

Cathedrals and parish churches are an expression of local pride. They are also symbols of the majesty of God, and give people a sense of religious wonder.

(Above) Notre Dame Cathedral, Paris. In medieval times, cathedrals took many years to build and were of the finest design and craftsmanship possible.

The Metropolitan Cathedral of Christ the King, Liverpool. This modern, Roman Catholic cathedral was opened in 1967. It was built in the round, with the altar in the centre, so that the congregation can be seated all round it.

Holy Innocents Church, Orpington. This is another example of a modern Roman Catholic church building. It has a striking exterior.

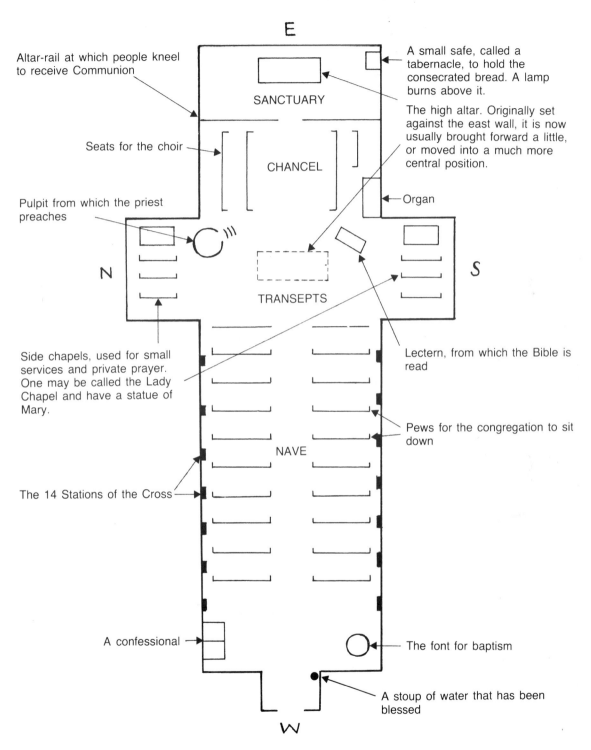

E

Altar-rail at which people kneel to receive Communion

A small safe, called a tabernacle, to hold the consecrated bread. A lamp burns above it.

The high altar. Originally set against the east wall, it is now usually brought forward a little, or moved into a much more central position.

SANCTUARY

Seats for the choir

CHANCEL

Organ

Pulpit from which the priest preaches

N

S

TRANSEPTS

Side chapels, used for small services and private prayer. One may be called the Lady Chapel and have a statue of Mary.

Lectern, from which the Bible is read

Pews for the congregation to sit down

NAVE

The 14 Stations of the Cross

A confessional

The font for baptism

A stoup of water that has been blessed

W

**Fig. 8.** The traditional plan of a medieval church

There are some exciting new designs in church buildings, but most churches you see will have been built on traditional lines, as shown in the diagram. About two hundred cathedrals and thousands of parish churches were built like this throughout Europe in the Middle Ages (thirteenth to fifteenth centuries). Remember that the whole of Europe at that time was Roman Catholic, divided into local areas, or parishes. A cathedral is the large church where the bishop has his official seat. (The word 'cathedral' comes from the Latin *cathedra*, which means 'seat'.) Later, some of these buildings were taken over by different denominations (e.g. Anglicans in England and Lutherans in Sweden); and some of the Protestants continued to build churches to the same design.

As you enter a Catholic church, you may notice a small bowl of water by the door, often carved into the stonework of a pillar or doorway. It is called a 'stoup'. Worshippers dip the fingers of their right hand into it and make the sign of the cross on themselves. You will usually find the font at the back of the church too, where babies are baptised. It is by the door, as a sign that they are entering into the Christian community. But some churches now place it at the front, to emphasise the belief that baptism brings the person fully into Church membership. When Catholics cross themselves with the holy water from the stoup, they may recall that the priest put the sign of the cross on them, in water, when they were baptised.

In the diagram (Fig. 8), no screen separates the people from the altar, and sometimes the altar-rail is also removed. In many churches the altar is brought forward so that the people can see and feel that they are involved with the priest as he celebrates the Mass. Originally, however, there would probably have been a 'rood screen' (Fig. 9) separating the chancel from the nave. This was made of wood and had an arch in the middle of it and a crucifix (the term used for a cross with the figure of Christ hanging on it) over the top of it. *Rood* was an old word for 'crucifix'. During the Middle Ages people could only see the priest celebrating Mass by looking through the arch in the screen or through little slits cut in the sides of the main chancel arch, called squints.

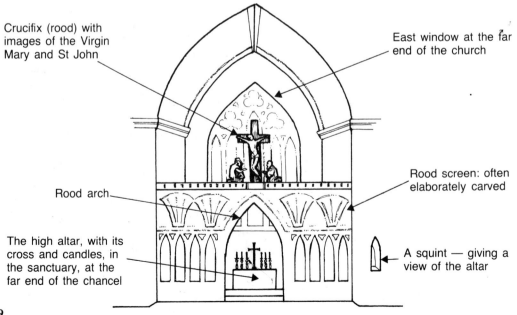

Crucifix (rood) with images of the Virgin Mary and St John

East window at the far end of the church

Rood screen: often elaborately carved

Rood arch

The high altar, with its cross and candles, in the sanctuary, at the far end of the chancel

A squint — giving a view of the altar

**Fig. 9**

Usually towards the back of a church you will see one or more confessionals. These are wooden cubicles divided into two sections. The priest sits in one part, and the person who has come to confess his or her sins kneels on the other side. The priest hears the person's confession through a small grill, and then gives advice and recommends that certain prayers should be said or things done. This is called the penance. There are many different designs of confessionals. Some are enclosed by curtains or doors.

1 Copy out the plan of a traditional church building and, in a key, explain what everything is used for.
2 Why do you think a traditional church building is in the shape of a cross?
3 A rood screen may have statues of the Virgin Mary and St John on either side of the crucifix. What event does this represent? Look up John 19:26–7, and describe it in your own words.
4 The rood screen was designed to cut off the people from the holiest part of the church, where the Mass was celebrated; just like the screen called an iconostasis in an Orthodox church.
(a) Why do you think this was done?
(b) Explain why the Roman Catholic Church no longer builds these screens and often brings the altar forward.

5 Design your own church building. Either draw a picture of what it would look like on the outside, or draw a plan of the inside, showing what you would have in it.
6 If you have ever visited a cathedral, explain how you felt when you were inside and looked about you.

# PRIESTS AND MINISTERS

A priest is a person who brings other people to God and makes him real for them. Catholics believe that Jesus Christ is the one true priest, and that the pope, the bishops and priests of the Church share in that work of Christ. The pope is called the Vicar of Christ – the one who stands in his place, representing him to the people. Bishops are put in charge of a number of churches and priests.

In the Catholic Church only men may become priests. This is done in the service of Ordination. Holy Orders is regarded as one of the seven sacraments. These are symbolic actions through which God is believed to be specially at work in people. In this sacrament, a bishop lays his hands on the man's head and gives him authority to preach, to administer the sacraments, and particularly to forgive sins. According to Matthew's Gospel, Jesus gave Peter the authority to forgive sins, and it is believed that this authority is passed on to all priests.

Although the man who is ordained retains his normal human weakness, he is given a spiritual authority which he did not have before, and which cannot be shared with those who are not ordained. He is to be Christ's representative on Earth, and as such is given great respect. Priests must remain unmarried, but some married men now become deacons. These are ministers who assist the priests in their work.

This famous statue of St Peter is in St Peter's, Rome. Copies of it can be seen in many Catholic churches. St Peter is usually shown holding a large key, as a sign of his authority to forgive sins. Matthew 16:19 is the basis for this tradition. Jesus says to Peter: 'I will give you the keys of the Kingdom of Heaven; what you forbid on earth shall be forbidden in heaven, and what you allow on earth shall be allowed in heaven.'

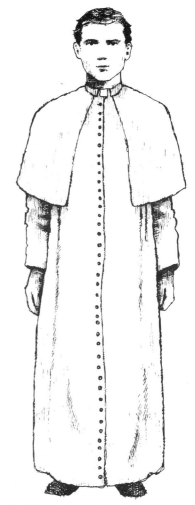

**Fig. 10.** Traditional dress for a Roman Catholic priest. Notice *'Roman' collar, *cassock, *cape.

Catholic priests usually wear what is called a 'Roman collar'. This shows a small portion of white collar surrounded by the black material of their shirt front. Sometimes they wear ordinary clothes, and on other occasions they may wear long black robes, called cassocks, sometimes with a short cape as well. The colour worn shows the rank a man has within the Church – white for the pope, purple for bishops, and black for most other priests. When priests celebrate Mass, they generally wear vestments, as illustrated. When taking part in a ceremony, a bishop will wear a special hat called a mitre (see photograph on p. 49). This is pointed, and represents the flames of fire which were said to have come upon the first disciples at Pentecost as a sign of the Holy Spirit. A bishop may also carry a crosier. This looks like a crook and shows that he is to be like a shepherd to his people.

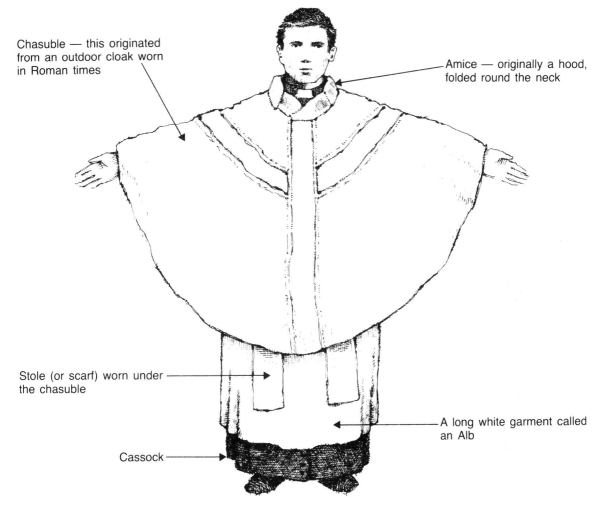

Chasuble — this originated from an outdoor cloak worn in Roman times

Amice — originally a hood, folded round the neck

Stole (or scarf) worn under the chasuble

A long white garment called an Alb

Cassock

**Fig. 11.** Vestments for celebrating Mass (the Holy Communion)

Monasticism is important in the Catholic Church, and there are a number of different orders for both men and women. From the sixth century come the Benedictines. They have a life which is balanced between prayer, study and manual work. Most of their work is done within a monastery or convent (for nuns).

Monks who go out travelling and preaching are called friars. Dominican Friars, started at the end of the twelfth century by St Dominic, are a preaching and teaching order. Because they wore black robes, the Dominicans were sometimes referred to as Black Friars. There are also the followers of St Francis – committed to a life of simplicity and poverty. They engage in preaching and charitable work. Although today Franciscans generally wear brown robes, they originally wore grey ones, and were called Grey Friars. Probably the most highly disciplined of the Catholic orders is the Jesuits. Founded by St Ignatius Loyola (1491–1556), they regard themselves as soldiers of the cross, and accept as absolute the authority of their superiors.

Nuns and monks can usually be recognised by the clothes they wear. They give up family life, and live in religious communities where they take the vows of poverty, chastity and obedience to the leader of their convent or monastery. Different monastic orders were set up for different purposes. Some monks and nuns live an enclosed life of prayer; others go out into the community. Many nuns are to be found teaching in convent schools, or running nursing homes.

1 Imagine that you have just been ordained as a Roman Catholic priest. Write a short letter to a non-Catholic friend, explaining what difference this has made to you.
2 Draw a diagram to show the three main responsibilities of a Catholic priest.
3 People confess their sins to a priest, in confidence, to be assured that God has forgiven them.
(a) If you have something on your conscience, is it better to talk about it with someone you trust, or to try to forget it? Explain your answer.
(b) Can you think of any advantages or disadvantages in telling a priest what you have done wrong, rather than telling God directly?

4 Draw the shape of a bishop's mitre. Then look up Acts 2:1–4 and, inside your picture, copy out the words which explain why the bishop's hat is this shape.

# PRAYER AND WORSHIP

The seven sacraments are the most important part of the religious life of Catholics. In a sacrament, God is believed to work through an outward, visible action to bring about an inward, spiritual benefit. The seven are: Baptism, Confirmation, Penance, Communion, Marriage, Holy Orders and the Sacrament of the Sick. (All of these are described at various places in this Part of the book.)

There are many aids to private prayer used by Catholics. One of these is to pray before the image of a saint, and perhaps light a candle, placing it on the rack which usually stands in front of the statue. This is not the same thing as worshipping the saint

– which would be idolatry, since Christians teach that God alone should be worshipped. The saint can be asked to pray to God for you, and to bring inspiration and help in times of need. In particular, Catholics use the Virgin Mary in this way. A very popular prayer is:

Hail Mary, full of grace,
The Lord is with thee,
Blessed art thou among women,
And blessed is the fruit of thy womb, Jesus.

This statue, with candles below it, is of St Antony of Padua in Italy. He was a Franciscan friar of the thirteenth century. He was famous for his preaching and is usually shown with a book or a lily, to symbolise his knowledge of the Bible. He is also shown here holding the child Jesus.

(a) How can you tell from this statue that St Antony was a friar?
(b) Why do you think he is shown holding the Holy Child when he lived 1200 years after Jesus?
(c) Why have some Roman Catholics lit candles by his statue?

Holy Mary, Mother of God,
Pray for us sinners, now
And in the hour of our death.

Catholic teaching about the Virgin Mary includes two things which Protestants do not share. The first is called the 'Immaculate Conception' of Mary. This means that from the time of her conception she was without sin of any kind, and was therefore fit to give birth to the Son of God. This is *not* the same thing as belief in the Virgin Birth, which means that Jesus was born to Mary while she was still a virgin. The second teaching is called the 'Bodily Assumption', and says that at the end of her life, Mary was taken bodily into heaven. Both of these ideas are found also in the Orthodox Churches, which call Mary the Mother of God and say that she is the first among saints. This reflects the devotion and respect paid to Mary in popular Catholic and Orthodox life.

Catholics sometimes say the rosary: a repetition of prayers (which includes the Hail Mary) to help them think about events in the lives of Jesus and Mary. They use a string of prayer-beads, turning them one by one through the fingers as each prayer is said; and these beads are also popularly called a rosary. It is an aid to concentration, as well as a way of counting off the prayers. Whereas in Protestant Churches it is most common for people to pray using their own words, Catholics find it useful to recite set prayers as well, of which the 'Hail Mary' given above is the most popular example.

Catholics, like the Orthodox, frequently make the sign of the cross on themselves, but they touch the left shoulder before the right one. When they enter the church building, they may dip their fingers into a bowl of holy water by the entrance and make the sign of the cross. They may also go down for a moment on to one knee as an act of worship before the cross or the high altar. This form of kneeling is called genuflexion, which means 'bending the knee'.

In the Middle Ages, it became popular to go on pilgrimages to places of religious importance. In Jerusalem, pilgrims followed the stages of Jesus' journey to his crucifixion and burial. This is now shown on the walls of churches in the form of fourteen pictures of the 'Stations of the Cross'. By moving round the church with prayers before each of these, people can make a token pilgrimage, following the events of Christ's death.

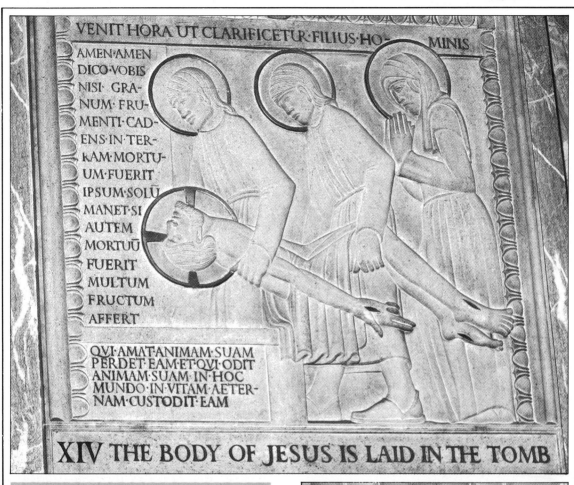

VENIT·HORA·UT·CLARIFICETUR·FILIUS·HOMINIS

AMEN·AMEN
DICO·VOBIS
NISI·GRA-
NUM·FRU-
MENTI·CAD-
ENS·IN·TER-
RAM·MORTU-
UM·FUERIT
IPSUM·SOLŪ
MANET·SI
AUTEM
MORTUŪ
FUERIT
MULTUM
FRUCTUM
AFFERT

QVI·AMAT·ANIMAM·SUAM
PERDET·EAM·ET·QVI·ODIT
ANIMAM·SUAM·IN·HOC
MUNDO·IN·VITAM·AETER-
NAM·CUSTODIT·EAM

XIV THE BODY OF JESUS IS LAID IN THE TOMB

(a) What are the pictures called which are shown here on the walls of this Roman Catholic church?
(b) They are not all visible here, but how many would you expect to find?
(c) What does the fourteenth one show?
(d) Some modern artists also add a picture of the Resurrection. Why do you think they want to do this?
(e) The description on the picture above is in an ancient language, used until recently for services in the Roman Catholic Church. What language is it? (See page 44.)

At one time people flocked to places like Santiago de Compostela in Spain to see the grave of the Apostle James, or to Canterbury to see where St Thomas Becket was murdered. Pilgrimages are still popular among many Christians. Roman Catholics in particular like to visit the Vatican in Rome which includes St Peter's and the pope's residence. They also visit pilgrimage centres such as Lourdes (where many healing miracles are claimed), and also Knock in Ireland and Fatima in Portugal where, as at Lourdes, visions of the Virgin Mary have been recorded.

In 1879 fifteen people from the village of Knock in Ireland claimed that the Virgin Mary had appeared to them. One hundred years later, Pope John Paul II knelt to pray at the Shrine of Our Lady of Knock in a special enclosure built on to the church. Knock is a pilgrimage centre. The second photograph shows the statue of the Blessed Virgin Mary being carried in procession.

(a) Try to find out more about the pilgrimage centre at Knock.
(b) Describe the procession in the picture in as much detail as possible.
(c) What religious benefits do you think Christians might get from going on a pilgrimage?
(d) Why do you think Mary is so popular as a person to whom Christians turn for help?

# THE MASS

The most important act of worship for Catholics is called the Mass, in which bread and wine are consecrated as the Body and Blood of Christ. This service is called the Liturgy in the Orthodox Churches and by other names, like Holy Communion, elsewhere. The name 'Mass' comes from the Latin word *missa*, meaning 'dismissal', used when the people are sent out at the end of the service. Whereas in the East the Orthodox Churches translated the service into the native languages of its people, the Roman Catholic Church (until 1963) used only Latin. This had the advantage of unity – a person could go into a Catholic church anywhere in the world and hear a familiar service. On the other hand, many people did not know much Latin, and therefore did not fully understand the meaning of all parts of the service.

Because it is such an important service, Catholics are encouraged to attend Mass every week, and priests usually say Mass every day. Before receiving the Sacrament, Catholics usually confess their sins to a priest and receive forgiveness. This sacrament is called Penance. The word means 'punishment' and refers to what the priest tells them to do to help them overcome their faults. Some priests prefer to speak of the Sacrament of Peace and Reconciliation. This is because, when Christians sin by going against God's laws, they hurt other people as well as making themselves unhappy. This sacrament is a way of asking God's help to put things right again. Traditionally, there are two categories of sin for Catholics – venial and mortal. The first is the result of minor matters, but the latter is more serious, and Catholics believe that if a person does not confess a mortal sin and receive forgiveness for it, then he or she is choosing to be separated off from God.

In the first part of the Mass there are readings from the Bible and prayers. Then comes the Offertory, when bread, wine and gifts of money from the people are taken to the altar, where the bread and wine are consecrated (made holy).

Christians believe that Christ died upon the cross as a sacrifice, which could overcome sin and bring people back into a right relationship with God. That one sacrifice cannot be repeated, but Catholics believe that in the Mass they can join with that sacrifice and receive its benefits, as Christ comes to them in the Communion (the consecrated bread and wine). Since Catholics see the Mass as joining in the sacrifice of Christ, the table upon which it is celebrated is called an altar, meaning that it is a place of sacrifice. Also, the consecrated bread is called the Host, which comes from the Latin word for a sacrificial victim.

In consecrating the bread and wine, the priest uses the words of Jesus at the Last Supper. Over the bread he says: 'Take this, all of you, and eat it: this is my body which will be given up for you.' And over the wine he says: 'Take this, all of you, and drink from it: this is the cup of my blood, the blood of the new and everlasting covenant. It will be shed for you and for all men so that sins may be forgiven. Do this in memory of me.' Catholics (like the Orthodox) take these statements in a literal way. They believe in 'transubstantiation' – literally, a change of substance. They believe that when the priest reads these words, the bread and wine actually become

Members of the congregation bring up the Offertory

Cardinal Hume, the Roman Catholic Bishop of England and Wales, celebrates Mass in his cathedral at Westminster.

(a) What words is he saying as he holds up the large priest's wafer (the bread)?
(b) When Jesus said these words, what event in his life was he predicting?

Roman Catholics believe that Christ is fully present in both the consecrated bread and the wine. It is therefore not necessary for people to receive both, and until recently ordinary people generally received only the bread. This is often in the form of a wafer (illustrated full-size in the corner of this photograph).

the Body and Blood of Christ. They still look and taste like bread and wine, but their inner substance, i.e. what they really are in themselves, has changed. Therefore Catholics treat the consecrated bread and wine with very great respect.

Traditionally, the ordinary people in the Catholic Church only received the consecrated bread, whereas the priest received both bread and wine. Many priests now give Communion to the people under both forms. The bread is usually a thin wafer, either placed directly into the mouth by the priest or into their hands, as the people kneel or stand before the altar.

Unlike the Orthodox Churches, the Catholic Church does not give Communion to very small children; although they may come to the altar-rail with their parents to receive a blessing. From the age of about seven years, children are usually allowed to receive Communion although they have not yet been confirmed (the sacrament in which they make their own commitment to the Church).

Recent changes in the Mass have brought the people much closer to the prayers and actions of the priest as he blesses the bread and wine. Firstly, the service is now in the ordinary language of the country. Secondly, it is now usual for the service to be conducted with the priest looking towards the people over the altar. This enables people to see what is happening, and also suggests the idea that both priest and people are gathered round a table together. In many churches the altar has been brought forward from the east wall (see Fig. 8) and placed centrally in the building.

Once the bread and wine have been consecrated, some of the bread can be set aside to be taken by the priest to those who are ill and therefore unable to attend the service. It is kept in church in a little box called a tabernacle. This is sometimes built into the wall of the sanctuary like a safe, or set on the altar itself. Whenever the consecrated bread is stored in it, a lamp is lit nearby, as a sign of Christ's presence.

1 Explain the meaning of 'transubstantiation'.
2 Design a diagram which illustrates the idea that every time the Mass is celebrated, in every place, it shares in the sacrifice of Christ on the cross.
3 (a) What reasons have been given in this section to explain why Christians take Communion?
(b) If you know any Christians who take Communion, ask them why they do this, and record their answers.
4 In the Orthodox Churches, everyone who is a member of the Church by baptism, however young, can have the consecrated bread and wine. In the Roman Catholic Church, children have to be taught about the Mass before they can receive their First Communion, usually at the age of seven. Which of these practices do you think is preferable? Give reasons for your answer.

# STAGES IN LIFE

**Baptism**
In the Roman Catholic Church, children are baptised at a font, with specially blessed water. A small bowl may be used, rather than a traditional font (as in the photograph). The water is sprinkled three times on their heads in the name of the Father, the Son and the Holy Spirit; and the baby is anointed before and after this with oil. Baptism is the means of becoming a member of the Church.

The parents are told that they must accept responsibility for bringing up their child in the Christian faith, and they are to be helped in this by godparents, whom they have chosen for this purpose. Both the parents and godparents are questioned about their own faith, to make sure that they understand and are ready for the task they have undertaken on behalf of the child.

If adults are baptised, they are sprinkled with water in the same way as children, but they make their own response to the questions about their faith, and they make their own act of commitment to follow it.

It is believed that baptism washes away sins, and gives a new spiritual birth as a child of God. A baby does not understand right from wrong, and therefore cannot have committed any sins as an individual, but baptism is still regarded as essential. This is because it is believed that ever since the disobedience of Adam in the Garden of Eden, humanity suffers from 'original sin' – something which a person is born with, not something which is done. At baptism, the effect of original sin is set aside, and any sins committed later in life can be forgiven if they are confessed.

The person who is baptised (or the parent or godparent on behalf of the child) is given a lighted candle. In the New Testament, Christ is described as the Light of the World, and the newly baptised person is therefore a child of light. He or she must 'shine as a light in the world'.

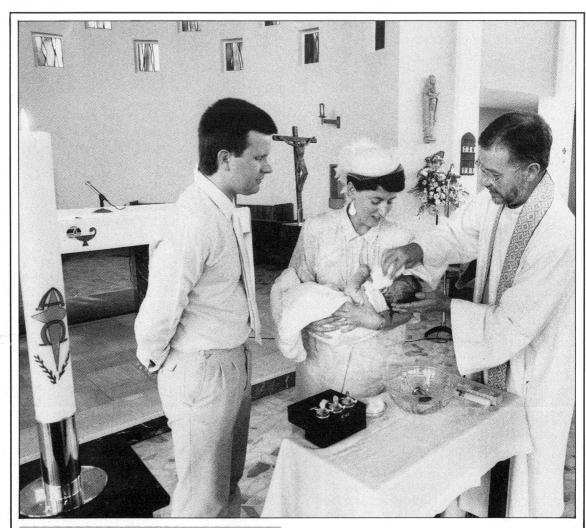

After reading the section on Baptism, describe this photograph in as much detail as possible.

48

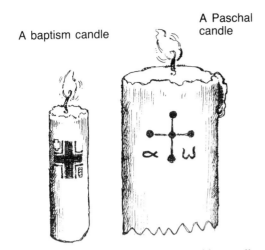

A baptism candle

A Paschal candle

**Fig. 12.** The Paschal candle is a large white candle which is brought into church on the eve of Easter Sunday. It is lit outside the church with a prayer such as this: 'May the light of Christ, rising in glory, banish all darkness from our hearts and minds.' Afterwards the small candles may be lit from this at baptism services.

## Confirmation

When young children are old enough to take responsibility for their own beliefs, they may be prepared for Confirmation (a 'making firm' in their faith). A bishop asks them if they turn to Christ, if they are sorry for their sins, and if they reject evil. He then lays his hands on each person's head and prays that he or she may receive the Holy Spirit. He makes the sign of the cross in oil on their heads and then, as he says 'Peace be with you', he gives each one a tap on the cheek with his hand. This is a sign that the person must be prepared to suffer hardship and discipline for the faith.

The bishop (wearing a mitre) makes the sign of the cross on the girl who is being confirmed. The woman standing beside her is her 'sponsor' — a member of the church who will encourage her in her Christian life.

## Marriage

Catholics regard marriage as a sacrament. It is holy, and of religious as well as personal importance for those who marry. In one of the prayers from a modern Catholic prayerbook (Rite of Marriage III) it says:

Love is man's origin
Love is his constant calling,
Love is his fulfilment in heaven.
The love of man and woman is made
holy in the sacrament of marriage,
and becomes the mirror of your
everlasting love.

The love of a husband and wife for one another is meant to express God's love for them. The family has been called the 'domestic church', and Catholics are taught to value family life. There is a rule that Catholic couples should not practise any artificial form of birth control. This is to make sure that every act of love between man and wife could possibly lead to the creation of new life. It has caused much debate among Catholics. Many who oppose it are concerned that the size of families should be limited, especially among those too poor to provide for all their children.

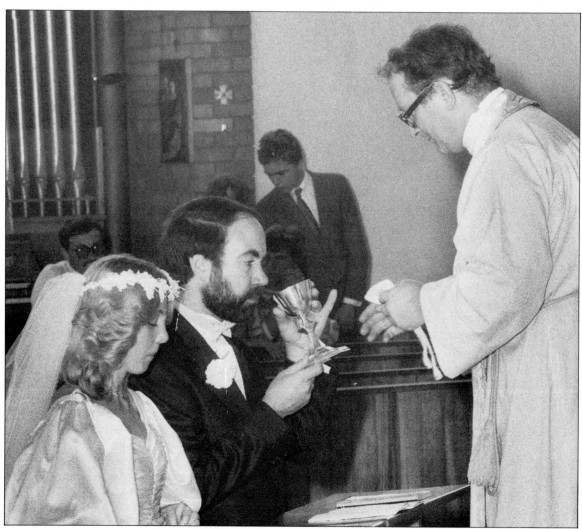

A Nuptial Mass — the bride and groom receive the bread and wine of Holy Communion.

At a Catholic wedding service, the couple make their promises to one another, give and receive a ring (or rings) and are blessed and joined in marriage by the priest. Then they sometimes choose to take Communion together as the first act of their married life. This part of the marriage is called the Nuptial Mass. It is not a necessary or legal requirement, but expresses the importance of marriage in the Catholic faith.

If a marriage breaks down, the Catholic Church does not accept civil divorce, but regards the couple as still being married in the sight of God. The only way in which they can separate and marry other partners is to show that there was some reason why their first marriage was not performed properly. For example, they might argue that there was something about themselves or their partner which they did not know when they made the promises of marriage, and which, if known, would have prevented the marriage from happening. This process of setting aside a marriage is called 'annulment'.

**Death**

There are two sacraments which Catholics believe to be of spiritual benefit to a person who is seriously ill and in danger of dying. The first is Penance. If the person is conscious, there should be an opportunity to make a confession to a priest and to receive absolution from all his or her sins. The second is the Sacrament of the Sick (also called Unction) which involves anointing with oil. This can be done at any time when a person is sick, but in practice it is generally reserved for those who are gravely ill. The oil for the anointing is blessed by the bishop each year during Holy Week (the week leading up to Easter) and then distributed among the priests and deacons of his diocese. Oil is a symbol of healing, and the prayers at this time ask for a person to receive physical healing, so as to recover, or spiritual healing, so that the person can be at peace as he or she approaches physical death.

Go forth upon your journey Christian Soul

Go in the name of God

Cards like this are sent to tell people that a Requiem Mass is taking place. The details are written inside.

The family of someone who has died may arrange a Requiem Mass – a service where special prayers are offered for the soul of the departed. After death, Catholics believe that the soul may not be ready to go to heaven, but may have to spend some time in what is called 'purgatory' – a place of training and preparation.

When the coffin is brought into a church building for the funeral service, the Paschal Candle used at Easter is placed by its head. This is to express the resurrection of Christ. The coffin is also sprinkled with holy water, which is a reminder of baptism and the entry into eternal life.

1 Design either a baptism or a wedding card, trying to show in both pictures and words its religious significance for Catholics.
2 (a) Do you think that it is right for parents to promise that they will bring up their children in their own religion?
(b) At what age should a young person be free to make his or her own decision on this?
3 Light is one of the symbols of baptism.
(a) Read Matthew 5:14–16 and explain what it says here about the followers of Jesus.
(b) What could it mean for someone to 'shine as a light in the world'?
4 Describe in your own words, or illustrate in some way, the ideas about married love given in the prayer in this section.
5 What comfort do you think it gives a person to do penance and receive the Sacrament of the Sick when close to death?

# FESTIVALS

**Advent Sunday**
This starts a period of over three weeks leading up to Christmas. It is a time of preparation and looking forward to the coming of Christ – both his birth in Bethlehem and also the belief that he will come again at the end of time. Advent calendars are sometimes used to mark off the days to Christmas, or an Advent candle is burned down a little each day during this season. It is also a time when there are Carol Services, with readings looking forward to Christmas.

**Christmas**
The birth of Christ is celebrated on 25 December, with traditional Christmas foods and giving of presents. Houses, and often churches, are decorated with Christmas trees and coloured lights. In churches you can

usually see a 'crib', which is a model of a stable, showing the scene of Jesus' birth. A popular service is Midnight Mass, which usually lasts from about 11.30 p.m. to 12.30 a.m. The people are there when Christmas begins so that the first thing they do on this joyful day is to take Communion.

**Epiphany**
Held on 6 January, this celebrates the showing of Christ to the whole world, expressed in the persons of the Wise Men. The word epiphany means to 'show forth'.

**Ash Wednesday**
This is the first day of Lent, the season leading up to Easter. It is a time of discipline and preparation to celebrate Easter. On Ash Wednesday, ash (made by burning the palm crosses from the previous year) is smeared on the foreheads of the people, in the shape of a cross. Being marked with ashes is a symbol of being sorry for your sins.

**Easter**
The events of Holy Week, the week leading up to Easter, are similar to those in the Orthodox tradition.
(i) Holy Week starts on Palm Sunday when palm crosses are blessed and distributed to the people.
(ii) On Maundy Thursday Christians remember the events of the night before Jesus died. At the Last Supper Jesus gave his disciples bread and wine to represent his body and his blood, so it is customary to receive Communion on this Thursday. John's Gospel tells us that Jesus washed the feet of his disciples as an example of humble service. The pope, like many other priests, washes the feet of chosen people on Maundy Thursday. *Maundy* comes from the Latin word for 'commandment'; for Jesus commanded his disciples to love one another.
(iii) On Good Friday three-hour services are held to remember the time Jesus hung on the cross.

Advent calendars have 'windows' — one to be opened each day from the 1st to the 24th December.

Try making your own. You will need one sheet of thin card with a Christmas scene painted on it. Draw 24 'windows' on this card and cut around three sides of each 'window' so that they can be opened. Number them 1 to 24. Stick a thicker piece of card of the same size underneath. Draw Christmas symbols on the spaces beneath the 'windows'.

(iv) Holy Saturday is a time of confession and for decorating the church in preparation for Easter Day. At an evening service a large candle is lit, which burns through all the services of the Easter season. It is called the Paschal candle (see p. 49).

(v) Easter Sunday is the most important festival of the Church, celebrating the resurrection of Jesus Christ. Frequent Masses are said on this day.

### Ascension Day
Coming forty days after Easter, this commemorates the New Testament story of Jesus being carried up into heaven. After reading the Gospel at Mass on this day, the Paschal candle is put out and the season of Easter is over.

### Pentecost
Celebrated (as its name means) fifty days after Easter, this recalls the coming of the Holy Spirit upon the disciples, and is seen as the birthday of the Church. It is often called Whitsunday (for White Sunday) because traditionally it was a time for people to be baptised, wearing white clothes.

Every Sunday is regarded as a festival, being the day of the week on which it is believed that Jesus rose from the dead. Friday, the day of the crucifixion, is regarded as a time of fasting and discipline. Catholics used to mark Friday by going without meat (or eating fish instead), but this is not a rule that everyone has to accept today.

Saints are important in the Catholic Church, and throughout the year there are days set aside to remember particular saints. Through the ages, specially holy Christians have been recognised as saints by the pope. Many of these were martyrs who died for their faith. The Saints' Days are often the days on which they died. Saints' Days are marked by special prayers and readings from the Bible at Mass. Churches are generally dedicated to a particular saint, and are referred to as, for example, St Paul's or St Peter's. That Saint's Day after whom the church is named is called the Patronal Festival, and may be celebrated with special services and other events.

1 What special events are there in the course of a year for you and your family? Make a list of the dates and events, noting briefly how you are likely to celebrate each of them.
2 Draw a diagram of a year (in twelve sections for the twelve months), and mark on it the festivals listed in this chapter.
3 Choose one of these festivals and try, through a drawing, to show what it means for the worshipper. Think of it as a poster which could be put up outside a church building to advertise the coming festival.
4 List (and illustrate if you wish) the traditional Christmas foods.
5 You hope that your close family and friends think about you every day. What then (apart from any presents) is the advantage of celebrating your birthday? Can you use the same argument for Saints' Days?
6 Do you know of a church which is named after a saint? Try to find out who the saint was.

# CHECK YOUR READING ON THE ROMAN CATHOLIC CHURCH

1 Who is believed to have founded the Church of Rome?
2 What title is given to the Bishop of Rome?
3 What are the four marks of the Church?
4 What is the traditional shape of a Catholic church building?
5 What do you find in a 'stoup'?
6 Which two saints are shown on either side of the crucifix on a 'rood screen'?
7 What is a confessional?
8 How is a priest ordained?
9 What colour are the robes worn by the pope?
10 A bishop's mitre is pointed. What does this shape represent?
11 Name an order of friars.
12 What are the seven sacraments?
13 Who confirms people?
14 What is the name of the sacrament which involves confession and absolution of sins?
15 Which is more serious, a venial or a mortal sin?
16 What is the 'Hail Mary'?
17 What is a rosary used for?
18 What do Fatima, Knock and Lourdes have in common?
19 What are the fourteen pictures around the walls of a church called?
20 What do Catholics call the service in which bread and wine are consecrated?
21 What is the minimum age at which Catholics can normally receive Communion?
22 What is kept in a tabernacle?
23 What does it mean if a marriage is annulled?
24 Which day is the beginning of Lent?
25 What are Saints' Days?

# PART 3
# The Protestant Churches

## WHEN, WHERE AND WHY

The Protestant Churches first came about as a result of protests against the Roman Catholic Church, made in the sixteenth century, in what is known as the Reformation.

Although there had been attempts at reform before this, the Reformation is thought of as starting in 1517, when a monk called Martin Luther posted on the door of his church ninety-five points for discussion (called the '95 Theses'). Luther was a professor at the university of Wittenburg in Germany, and he was prepared to argue against what he saw as

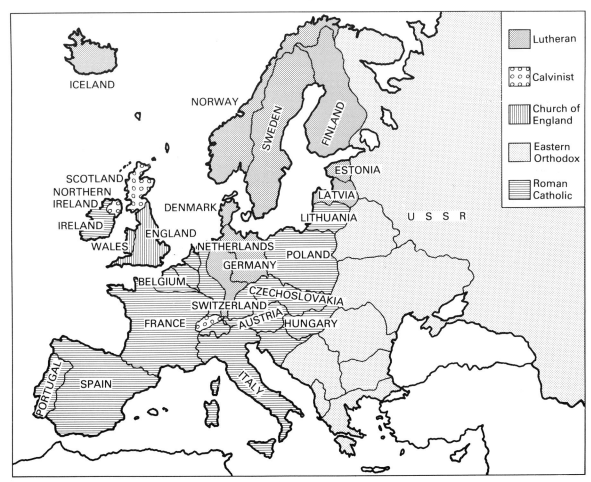

**Map 4.** How Protestantism has changed the face of Christianity in Europe

the corrupt practices of the Church. He was provoked into doing this by the arrival of a representative of the pope, collecting money for the rebuilding of the great church of St Peter in Rome by selling indulgences (certificates which claimed to give people freedom from God's punishment for sins they had committed).

Luther argued that:

(i) a person could be set right in the eyes of God through faith alone, not by buying an indulgence or by performing some special religious duty;

(ii) all true believers were priests and could pray to God directly for the forgiveness of their sins;

(iii) the final authority for Christians was the Bible rather than the Church, and it was the duty of every Christian to interpret the Bible for himself or herself.

Luther's views were condemned by Rome, and he was excommunicated – that is, he was expelled from the Church. As a result of this, many Christians separated from the Roman Catholic Church and followed Luther's teachings. By his death in 1546, some of southern Germany, most of northern Germany, Norway, Sweden, Denmark and the smaller states around the Baltic were already following the Lutheran form of Christianity. After a long struggle, it was decided that each area should follow the form of Christianity used by its ruler.

More radical reforms were underway in Geneva in Switzerland, under the leadership of John Calvin. Calvinism accepted only what was in the Bible, and rejected all other Catholic practices. It was a very strict form of religion, and no images were allowed in churches, not even a cross. The ministers were called presbyters, which gave the name Presbyterianism to this form of organisation. John Knox took Calvin's ideas to Scotland where Presbyterianism was to become the State Church – the only country where this has happened. Calvinism also spread to France, Holland, Strasbourg and some parts of southern Germany.

Because Henry VIII established the Church of England, breaking away from the authority of the pope, the British monarch is its 'Supreme Governor' and the Archbishop of Canterbury is its religious leader. Here they are together in 1985: Queen Elizabeth II and Archbishop Robert Runcie.

In England, Henry VIII wanted his marriage to Catherine of Aragon annulled in order that he might marry Ann Boleyn. The pope refused this, and Henry therefore took the step of separating off the Church of England from the rest of the Catholic Church. Henry was not a reformer, and had previously received the title 'Defender of the Faith' for his book attacking Luther. But he now made himself the Head of the Church of England, and no longer accepted the authority of the pope.

Under his successor Edward VI, there was a move towards the reformers' point of view. Then came Queen Mary who, in a reign of only four years, insisted on the Catholic faith once more, and ordered 283 people to be burnt at the stake for Protestant beliefs. It was only after

Elizabeth I came to the throne in 1558 that a Prayer Book was devised which combined both Protestant and Catholic ideas. The Church of England (also called the Anglican Church, and now found throughout the world) is therefore half-way between Catholic and Protestant – keeping many of the traditions of the Catholic Church, but also taking ideas from the reformers.

Some Christians were dissatisfied with the Church of England under Elizabeth I, and wanted it purified of Catholic practices. They became known as Puritans. During the years that followed, some of them formed what became known as the Free Churches. They were also called Non-Conformist Churches, as they did not conform to the Church of England. A Free Church is a Protestant Church which is not controlled by the State. In 1572 the first English Presbyterian Church was set up in Wandsworth, London (chiefly because its members objected to priests wearing special vestments for services). In 1580 a group of Christians in Norwich formed a Congregational Church. They organised themselves, elected leaders from their own congregation, and argued that the Church should be restricted to those who were committed to the Christian religion, and not open to all who happened to be born in a Christian country.

Puritans suffered persecution, with punishments which included branding, cutting off an ear and life-imprisonment. Between 1620 and 1640 about 20,000 of them fled to North America, seeking religious freedom. Among them were the Pilgrim Fathers who established Congregationalism in New England in 1620.

An American family celebrates Thanksgiving Day with the traditional turkey followed by pumpkin pie. This is one of the most important festivals in the USA and comes on the fourth Thursday of November.

It celebrates the ingathering of the first harvest by the Pilgrim Fathers — and therefore their survival in their new homeland.

Some argued that babies should not be baptised, but only adults who could understand and agree to follow the Christian religion. These became Baptists. The first Baptist Church started in Holland in 1609 among a group of English people who had fled there to escape persecution. In 1639 they crossed the Atlantic to North America to found the Baptist community of Rhode Island.

It was the middle of the seventeenth century before these Churches could worship openly in England. For some time, discipline in the Church of England had been very poor – many priests were regularly drunk or involved in scandal, and some parishes had no priest at all. This was criticised by the Puritans and it encouraged many serious-minded people to join their Churches.

In 1652 the Society of Friends was started by George Fox. They were called 'Quakers', probably because Fox said that a judge, in whose court he had to appear, should quake at the presence of God. They refused to swear on the Bible, claiming that the truth itself was as holy as that book. For them, religion was a matter of following their personal convictions, not of obeying outward religious rules. They were pacifists, refusing to fight because they believed that no good could come from violence. A Quaker called William Penn, persecuted like many others, established Pennsylvania (meaning 'Penn's woods') in North America, and in 1682 founded the city of Philadelphia (meaning 'brotherly love'), a place of religious freedom.

In the eighteenth century another major denomination gradually broke away from the Church of England. Led by John and Charles Wesley, a group gathered together in Oxford to study and pray in a serious or 'methodical' fashion. They became known as 'Methodists' and formed groups within Church of England parishes, holding weekly meetings for study and prayer, and encouraging people to attend their parish church. Gradually, partly as a result of their

own success and partly because of opposition from the established Church, they broke away to form the Methodist Church.

Because John Wesley's style of preaching was different from theirs, many of the Anglican churches closed their doors to him, and so he preached out in the open. It is estimated that he preached over 40,000 sermons as he travelled around the country. This picture shows people reacting emotionally to his appeal for personal commitment to Christ.

Other important groups started in the nineteenth century. The Salvation Army, founded by William Booth in 1865, had a military type of organisation. Its members preached and did social work. They rejected all sacraments, practised strict moral discipline and made public statements of their faith.

All of the groups mentioned so far started in Europe, but other denominations have come from Africa and America. The most important of these are the Pentecostal Churches. Starting in the early years of the twentieth century, Pentecostalism came out of a tradition of dramatic preaching of the

Catherine Bramwell-Booth, granddaughter of William and Catherine Booth, the founders of the Salvation Army, who died in 1987 aged 104. She was a Commissioner in the Salvation Army and is shown here in uniform.

Gospel. Pentecostalists place great importance on the 'gifts of the Spirit' which Jesus' first disciples were described as receiving at Pentecost. The gift of 'speaking in tongues', or in a strange language, is taken as a sign that a person has been baptised in the Holy Spirit. There are many Pentecostal Churches, the largest of them is the Assemblies of God, formed in 1914 in America.

Notice that, because Protestants claim that every person has a duty to study and interpret the Bible, there are bound to be disputes about its meaning. This has led to the further splitting up of Protestant Churches.

1 List the denominations mentioned in this section. Next to each of them note briefly what each of the 'names' stands for (e.g. Why are Baptists called Baptists?). You can answer this question with an illustrated diagram if you prefer.

2 Two kinds of denominations have been described in this section. Some (the Lutheran Church or the Church of England, for example) offer membership to the very young, and many people belong to them to some extent. Others (Congregationalists and Baptists, for example) limit membership to those who are committed to the Christian religion. Organise a class debate, with half of the pupils chosen to represent one point of view, and half the other. Take time to think of the arguments for one position and against the other before the debate starts.

# BUILDINGS

At the Reformation, the Protestants believed that all devotion before an image or a statue was in danger of becoming idolatry. Their one concern was that all trimmings should be removed so that an uncluttered form of Christianity could be established, based on their interpretation of the Bible and offering a direct relationship with God through Christ. Therefore there was widespread destruction of religious images. If you look round churches and cathedrals that date from before the sixteenth century, you may see statues which have been partly destroyed, with faces disfigured or heads removed. There may also be small alcoves in the walls which now remain empty, but once had statues in them.

In some places, older buildings were taken over by Protestants and adapted for their own use. They sometimes plastered or painted over the images on the walls. Many Anglican churches therefore follow the same pattern as the traditional Roman Catholic design shown on p. 36 (in most cases the rood screen will have been removed).

59

Sixteenth-century Protestants destroying images in a church in the Netherlands.

(a) Choose one of the people in the picture and describe what he or she is doing.
(b) Now imagine you are that person. Describe your feelings and the reasons for your actions.

When Protestants built their own meeting places for worship they were of a different design. They are often called 'chapels', and although they vary from one denomination to another, the diagram in Fig. 13 of a Free Church chapel contains features commonly found. The walls are plain, and there are no side chapels such as you might find in a Catholic church. The building is likely to be dominated by the pulpit, from which the minister preaches. This reflects the importance given to the preaching of sermons within the Protestant tradition. There will often be a gallery round three sides of the building, enabling the maximum number of people to see and hear the preacher.

In front of the pulpit is a plain wooden table for celebrating the Communion. In front of that, for denominations which practise 'Believers' Baptism', is the

A simple Baptist chapel in Derbyshire

60

baptistery. This is a pool which is usually drained and covered over when not in use. It needs to be large enough to accommodate the person to be baptised, with the minister and perhaps one other person to assist (see p. 71).

When there is a choir and an organ, they are set to one side or at the back of the building, so that they can help with the singing without intruding into the service.

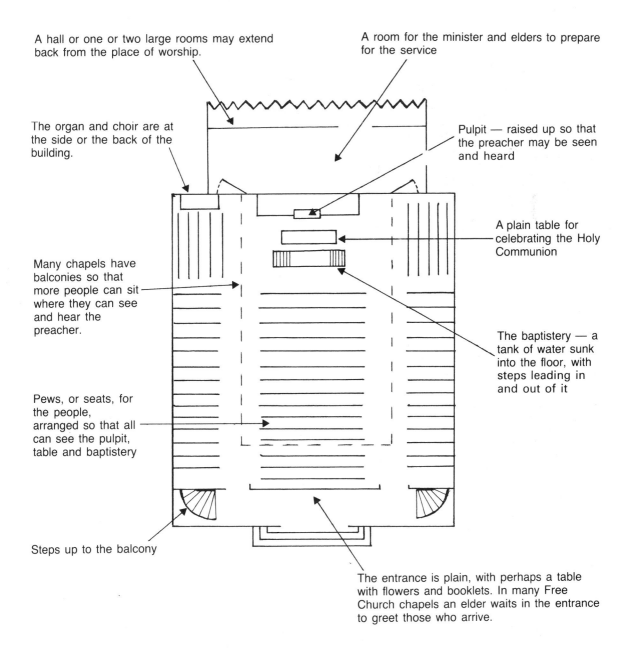

A hall or one or two large rooms may extend back from the place of worship.

A room for the minister and elders to prepare for the service

The organ and choir are at the side or the back of the building.

Pulpit — raised up so that the preacher may be seen and heard

A plain table for celebrating the Holy Communion

Many chapels have balconies so that more people can sit where they can see and hear the preacher.

The baptistery — a tank of water sunk into the floor, with steps leading in and out of it

Pews, or seats, for the people, arranged so that all can see the pulpit, table and baptistery

Steps up to the balcony

The entrance is plain, with perhaps a table with flowers and booklets. In many Free Church chapels an elder waits in the entrance to greet those who arrive.

**Fig. 13.** Plan of a Free Church chapel

The 'mercy seat' in a Salvation Army citadel

1 (a) What do you consider to be the two most distinctive features of the church building shown in Fig. 13?
(b) What do these two features tell you about Protestant Christianity?
2 Draw two columns and list the advantages and disadvantages of having a plain and simple place of worship (rather than one which is very decorative and with lots of images).
3 Do you think it might be possible to design a place of worship which could be used successfully by more than one of the major branches of Christianity? If so, draw a plan of it. What would be your chief problems with this? What objections might you receive from each of the traditions?

Because the Salvation Army is run on military lines, its places of worship are called citadels. A citadel is a fortress from which an army can go out. In the front of the main worship area of the citadel is a stage on which the band sits, and in the centre of this is set a lectern for Bible readings and preaching. In front of the stage there is a long bench, called the 'mercy seat'. Towards the end of the service, people are invited to come forward and kneel at it if they feel in need of help, or if they want to make any important decision about their lives. People who come to the 'mercy seat' are then attended to individually, being given advice and help.

The simplest form of building is that of the Society of Friends (Quakers). They use a plain room with chairs arranged, generally in a circle or rectangle, around a table. On it there stands a Bible, and perhaps a vase of flowers, but there is no further decoration of any kind (see p. 67).

# PRIESTS AND MINISTERS

Luther rejected the idea that some Christians are called to be specially holy and that people need priests to bring them to God through the sacraments. He taught that priesthood belonged to all believers, because Jesus had made it possible for people to approach God directly in prayer and receive his forgiveness.

For practical purposes, Protestant Churches need to have leaders of some sort to organise services and other activities; but these are not called priests, to avoid the idea that they have a special relationship with God, different from other Christians. They may be called ministers, because they minister to, or serve, the people of their church. Or they may be called pastors (*pastor* means 'shepherd' in Latin), because they are like shepherds caring for their sheep. They are only ministers for as long as they are doing that work, unlike a Catholic priest, who remains a priest after ordination whether or not he is practising as one.

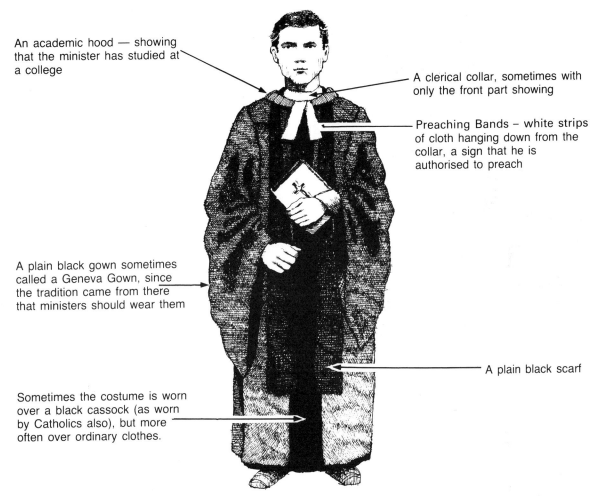

An academic hood — showing that the minister has studied at a college

A clerical collar, sometimes with only the front part showing

Preaching Bands – white strips of cloth hanging down from the collar, a sign that he is authorised to preach

A plain black gown sometimes called a Geneva Gown, since the tradition came from there that ministers should wear them

A plain black scarf

Sometimes the costume is worn over a black cassock (as worn by Catholics also), but more often over ordinary clothes.

**Fig. 14.** A Free Church minister.
Free Churches do not have fixed rules about what a minister should wear. This illustration gives some of the possibilities. Some ministers do not use any of these special clothes, but will conduct services in their ordinary dress. See how the Protestant ministers are dressed in the photographs on pages 65 and 74.

Calvin, following the example of the New Testament, went one step further than the Lutheran Church. Calvinist churches are 'presbyterian' because each church is run by a group of elders from among its congregation (the Greek word *presbyter* means 'elder'). They appoint the pastor and assist him in running the church, although he leads the worship and preaches.

When the Church of England divided off from Rome, it retained many of the features of Roman Catholicism, including the ordination of priests by bishops. Under Edward VI, priests were allowed to marry, like Protestant ministers. Some branches of the Anglican Church outside England now ordain women as priests. Some oppose this, because they say that a priest is meant to

The woman deacon here can baptise but is not allowed to celebrate Holy Communion. This is because the Church of England, like the Orthodox and Roman Catholic Churches, does not have women priests. Many people disagree with this.

Why do you think there is such a strong movement today to allow women to become priests?

Many smaller churches cannot afford to have full-time ministers, and are led by men and women who also have to do other work to make a living. Quakers choose to have no ministers at all. The whole congregation comes together in worship, and anyone can contribute.

Many Protestants believe that it is unnecessary (or even wrong) for a person to leave the normal concerns of life and enter a monastery or convent. At the Reformation, monasteries were emptied. Luther himself ceased to be a monk, married an ex-nun and had five children. Today, however, there are some religious communities among Protestants. The Anglican Church shares some Catholic Orders, having both Benedictines and Franciscans. There are also some communities among Protestants in which families share a common life together. Some communities go beyond the denominational boundaries (see the section 'The Ecumenical Movement').

1 Explain what is meant by the 'priesthood of all believers'.
2 Make two columns and list all the differences between Catholic priests and Protestant ministers.
3 After the Anglican Church broke away from Rome, it allowed its priests to get married. Do you think this was a sensible reform or not? Explain your answer.

represent Christ, who was a man. Most Protestants accept that both men and women can serve as ministers. In the Church of England, women can be ordained as deacons, who assist priests with their work.

Ministers of national Churches – like the Anglican Church in England, or the Lutheran Church in Sweden – generally serve the whole of the community within which they live. A minister of a Free Church, by contrast, is usually limited to looking after the members of his or her own church.

The Salvation Army is different again. Since it is run like an army, its commands come from the General at the top, and its full-time workers are officers of various ranks. All members of the Salvation Army wear uniforms (see pp. 59 and 62).

# PRAYER AND WORSHIP

Daily private prayer is very important for most Christians, but they also meet together for services. The Protestants at the Reformation believed that reading the Bible, interpreting it, and preaching from it, should be the most important parts of public worship. The sermon became the longest part of each service, delivered from a high pulpit, in a central position in the

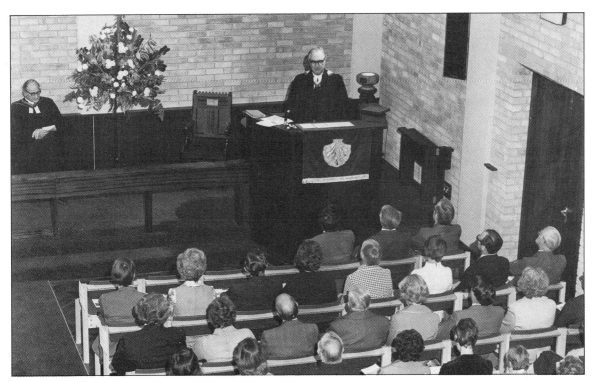

A modern Methodist church in Hayes, Middlesex.
Preaching the sermon still plays an important part in
Protestant services.

church. From here the preacher could make
a direct and personal appeal to his listeners,
telling them the 'good news' that Jesus
Christ died that their sins might be forgiven.

Although most Protestant Churches
celebrate the Communion Service in one
form or another, the tradition of Bible-based
worship has continued. Anglican churches
(Church of England) usually have morning
and evening services on a Sunday, which
consist of hymns, prayers, readings from the
Bible, a statement of faith (saying the Creed
together) and a sermon.

Free Churches have similar services, but
without the Creed and often without any set
forms of prayer. In almost all forms of
Protestant worship there is opportunity for
free (or 'extempore') prayer. This means
that the person praying (in public at a
service or in private) will use his or her own
words to ask God for something or to give
thanks.

Music plays an important part in
Protestant worship (as it does also in the
Orthodox and Catholic traditions). Luther
himself wrote hymns which are still used
today, as did Charles Wesley, the brother of
John. Hymns are easily remembered and
can be used to teach about the Christian
religion. In some Churches (especially
Pentecostal Churches) choruses take the
place of the more formal hymns. They are
often accompanied by instruments such as
electric guitars, trombones and cymbals.
People may clap their hands and dance as
they sing, to express their praise.

Some Churches make a direct and very
strong appeal to those who have come to
the service but are not yet full members of
the Church. There may be a call for people
to make a personal commitment to Christ.
These services are often fairly
demonstrative, with people crying, or calling
out with joy. For many Protestants, the

inner feeling of having been personally saved by Christ is the mark of true conversion. Christian conversion means that a person has come to a 'turning point' in his or her life, is sorry for past sins and wants Jesus to be his or her guide from then on. People may describe such a moment of emotional commitment and joy as being 'born again' in Christ.

There are some Christians who particularly claim to feel the power of the Holy Spirit upon them. They call themselves Charismatics, and are most often found in Pentecostal Churches. Both these names refer to Pentecost, when the Church first started. At this festival, the first disciples of Jesus are said to have felt the power of God's Spirit upon them, giving them the courage to go out and start preaching. The New Testament tells of the various 'gifts' (*charismata* – in Greek) that the Spirit gave them. These gifts can be found in Charismatic services today: praising God in strange languages (called 'speaking in tongues'); interpreting what others have said; prophesying – speaking God's message; and laying hands on sick people to cure them. Of these, the 'speaking in tongues' often appears most strange to outsiders. It seems that when worshippers can no longer find words to express their love for God, they let themselves go, and bubble over with a language of praise which they do not understand.

Notice that there is little reference in Protestant worship to the saints. This is because they believe that all prayer should be made directly to God through Christ, and that it does not need the help of any other human person, however holy.

The Catholic Church bases its worship on seven sacraments. Luther himself, and the Anglican Church, continued to use all of these, but a majority of Protestants accept

Choose six words to try to describe the atmosphere at this act of worship.

The Friends Meeting House, Esher — built in 1797. Everyone at the Meeting is considered equal, but the clerk, who sits facing the others, brings the Meeting to a close and reads out the notices. The other person with her in this photograph is her assistant. Children usually attend the Meeting for worship for only about ten minutes, since it is considered too long for them to sit in silence for the whole time. They are looked after in another room.

(a) How easy do you find it to remain silent for a long time?
(b) Is it easier to be silent with a friend or with a stranger (assuming that you do not *need* to say anything)?
(c) Why do people sometimes describe silences as 'embarrassing'?
(d) What are the benefits of setting aside times of silence?

only two – Baptism and Holy Communion. This is because these are the two which are specifically commanded by Jesus in the New Testament. Quakers and the Salvation Army have no sacraments at all, because they want to emphasise the inner meaning of religion rather than its outward ceremonies.

Quakers (The Society of Friends) probably represent the simplest form of worship. Their Meeting for Worship starts when the first person enters the room and sits down. It continues in silence, but from time to time one of the Friends present may feel that the Holy Spirit is prompting him or her to say something – a reading, a

prayer or a personal story or comment. Gradually the group of people experience an atmosphere of peace and worship as, in the silence, they think about the few things that have actually been said. Sometimes nothing is said at all. This does not matter, since Quakers believe that God speaks directly to each human individual in that silence, and that he is to be discovered within yourself, not in external words or actions.

This is in contrast to many other Churches, where people sing, clap, shake tambourines and sway in time to the music. Protestant worship includes a great variety of religious actions and emotions.

1 Write out a Christian hymn or chorus and explain the meaning of at least one part of it. Your teacher may wish to give it to you, or you may be able to choose one for yourself.
2 Look up 1 Corinthians 12:4–11 and list the gifts of the Spirit that are recorded there from verse 8 onwards. You should find nine in all.
3 Draw a diagram or three simple line drawings to show the differences between the worship of Anglicans, Protestants and Quakers.
4 Some people use music and dance in their worship, while others prefer to sit quietly.
(a) Which of these do you prefer?
(b) Explain why.
(c) What does each way suggest about the religious beliefs of the people who follow it?

# HOLY COMMUNION

The service of Holy Communion may also be called the 'Eucharist' (from the Greek, meaning 'thanksgiving'), the 'Lord's Supper' or the 'Breaking of Bread'. 'Holy Communion' expresses the idea that Christians are joined together in a community, with Christ, by sharing the bread and wine.

The service is made up of two parts (like the Orthodox and Catholic services). The first is the Ministry of the Word, which has Bible readings and prayers in order to prepare the people to receive their Communion. In the second part, bread and wine are taken and blessed, following the actions of Jesus at the Last Supper, and then shared among the people, as Jesus did among his disciples.

The main difference between the Catholic

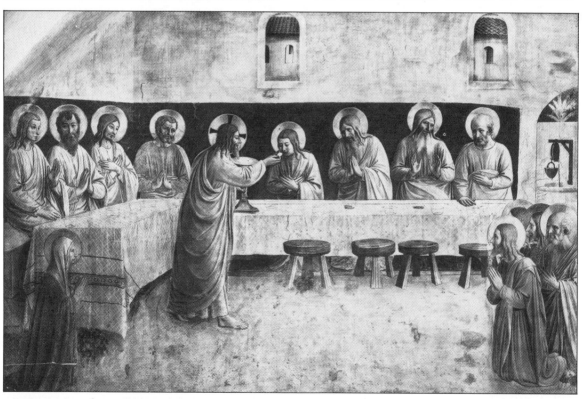

This painting is of the Last Supper, from which the Holy Communion service has come. The artist shows Jesus giving his disciples bread and wine, like a priest or minister giving Communion.

and Protestant branches of the Church is in what they believe happens when the bread and wine are blessed.

Luther believed that the bread and wine, while staying bread and wine, were *also* the Body and Blood of Christ, since Jesus had said 'this is my body' and 'this is my blood'. Notice that this was different from the Catholic belief. For Catholics, the bread and wine might look the same, but in fact they were now *only* the Body and Blood of Christ. Luther said that they were both things at once. This is a difficult idea to grasp! Think of a lump of stone. It is carved into a statue. Is it then both a lump of stone *and* a statue, or is it only a statue?

The biggest difference of interpretation came with the Calvinists. They said that the bread and wine did not change at all when they were blessed. The Communion Service was a memorial of Jesus' death on the cross, and the bread and wine were only symbols, representing Christ. Anything else could be seen as superstitious. Jesus had told his followers to share bread and wine in memory of him, and it should be done as simply as possible. This is the view taken by most Protestant denominations.

The most important idea of the Reformation was that people were justified in the sight of God through faith in Christ, not through trying to be religious. Everyone had sins that deserved punishment, and only God could forgive them. Sharing in the Communion Service was a sign of God's love and forgiveness, but if a person did *not* have faith, then no amount of taking part in the service would make any difference.

Protestants give Communion in both bread and wine, some using normal leavened bread and others using thin wafers. In some churches people come forward one by one to receive Communion, taking a piece of bread and sipping from the cup of wine. In others there are individual glasses of wine, so that everyone can have their Communion together at the same moment. (This 'wine' is often grape juice, because many Protestants do not drink alcohol.)

Separate glasses all together, or a single cup one at a time — which do you think best expresses the meaning of the Communion? Give your reasons.

In most Protestant Churches today there is a tendency to have Communion more frequently than in the past. Holy Communion has become the most important service in the Anglican Church and is celebrated every week, often several times. Free Churches generally celebrate it once a month but, at one time, many celebrated it only every three months. They were afraid that it would become a thoughtless custom if they did it too often.

As well as the Communion services in a church building, many groups of Christians use a short form of Communion when they meet together for prayer in one another's houses, and it can be done quite informally.

Now that the Catholic Church uses the ordinary language of the people, rather than Latin for the Mass, the different forms of Communion Service are more like one another, and in some cases it may be difficult to tell the difference between a Catholic and an Anglican celebration.

The important thing to remember is that for Protestants the Communion Service is a reminder of something (the death of Jesus,

69

and the love and forgiveness shown through him), but for Catholics, the Mass makes Christ really present among them. Catholics believe that the Mass actually does something *now*, but Protestants believe the Breaking of Bread points to something which has already been done.

1 Why do you think this service is sometimes called the 'Lord's Supper'? What event is this recalling?
2 Look back at the passage about the statue and the lump of stone.
   (a) How would you answer the question there? Can you give a reason for your choice?
   (b) Would you treat it differently if you thought it was a statue rather than a lump of stone?
3 Explain in your own words the main difference between Protestant and Catholic views of the Communion.
4 Explain why Protestants tend to take Communion less often than Catholics.

# STAGES IN LIFE

## Baptism
Who should be counted as a member of the Church? When babies are baptised, they become Christian without being able to make the decision for themselves, or to understand anything about the religion. Parents and godparents make promises on their behalf; but many who are baptised as babies do not practise the Christian religion when they grow up. Some Protestant Churches continue to baptise babies, but many baptise only those who have become believers. They may have a service of thanksgiving and dedication for the newborn child, but they wait for the child to grow up before they offer it baptism.

Believers' baptism, as it is called, is practised by many smaller denominations today, as well as by the Baptist Churches. It is a very important sacrament, obeying the New Testament command to 'believe and be baptised'. The person to be baptised makes a statement of his or her faith, and is ducked under water in the name of the Father, Son and Holy Spirit. Usually this is done in a baptistery (a tank of water sunk into the floor of the church), but it may be done anywhere where there is enough water. Sometimes it is done outside in a river. This follows the tradition of John the Baptist, who baptised people in the River Jordan. Jesus himself was baptised by him.

It is important in such baptisms that there is enough water for the person to be completely immersed. This symbolises being drowned to one's old life, or buried in the waters of baptism, before rising up afresh to a new life as a Christian. Baptism is therefore a sign of rebirth. The person being baptised has his or her sins forgiven and is born into the family of Christ. Some Christians speak about being 'born again' when they refer to the moment when they dedicated themselves to Christ. About one third of all adults in the United States describe themselves as 'born again Christians'.

In Charismatic churches, a person is said to be baptised in the Spirit when he or she starts to display the signs (like the speaking in tongues) which are taken to be the Holy Spirit at work. This is a moment when the believer feels that God is active in a very personal way, setting him or her apart from those who are Christian in name only. So these Christians speak of baptism in the Spirit, as well as baptism in water.

## Marriage
There are two parts to any marriage service. The first is a legal formality, and it can be performed in a Registry Office rather than in a church. The couple state that they want to marry one another and that there is no legal reason why they may not do so. They sign a marriage register in the presence of witnesses, and are given a certificate to prove that they are married. Some ministers are licensed to conduct

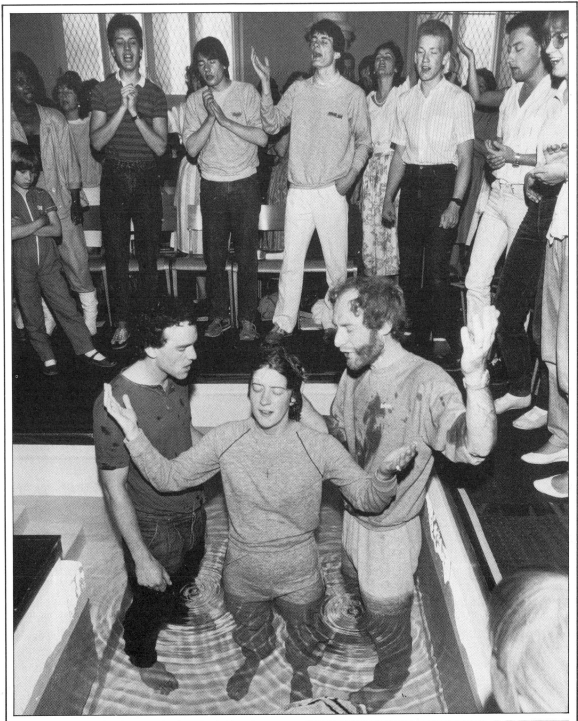

The woman here is about to be baptised. People are singing and praying all around her.

Imagine you are any one of the people in this photograph. What might you be praying at this moment?

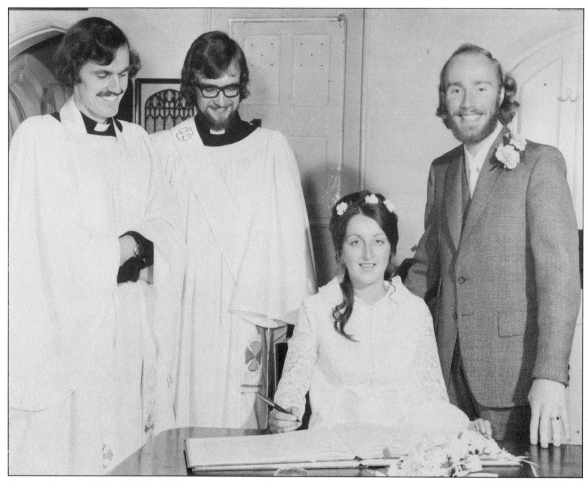

The signing of the Register takes place at the end of a Church of England wedding, where the priest acts as registrar. The other clergyman (with his stole tied across his body) is a deacon, who may only assist with the service.

marriages and to issue marriage certificates. Their church buildings are also licensed so that the marriage may be performed there. This is true of all Church of England priests and churches, because this is the State Church. Where a minister is not licensed, a registrar is present at the service. He or she is there to witness the statements that the couple make and to superintend the signing of the registers.

The other part of the marriage service consists of the promises that the couple make to one another, and the prayers for the blessing of God upon their life together.

This may be separated from the legal part – a couple can go to a Registry Office for the legal marriage, and then go on to a church for the religious ceremony. This sometimes happens in those churches which do not allow divorced people to remarry and to make new marriage promises to their second partner, but which will offer to bless the second marriage. The rules about this vary from one Church to another.

Most wedding ceremonies follow the same pattern. Promises are made by bride and bridegroom, and a ring is given to the bride, or rings are exchanged. The simplest form of service is that used by Quakers. At some point during the service the couple stand and each will say:

> Friends, I take this my Friend
> . . . .[name] to be my wife/husband, promising through divine assistance to be unto her/him a loving and faithful husband/wife so long as we both on Earth shall live.

The couple then sign a certificate with these words on it, and it is witnessed by at least two of those present. Notice the term 'Friend'. Quakers are called 'The Society of Friends' and refer to one another as 'Friend'.

### Death

A person who is seriously ill may be visited by the minister or other members of the church. Prayers and readings from the Bible may be shared, and in some churches the person may have 'the laying on of hands'. The minister may put his hands on the person's head, or on the part of the body that is causing the illness, with prayers for healing. Some Protestants may want to confess their sins if they know that they are near to death, but others regard this as a personal matter between themselves and God, and do not make confession in front of a minister.

Protestants may be either buried or cremated. When the funeral service is to be followed by cremation, the whole ceremony may take place in the chapel of a crematorium, or else the main service is held in the person's own chapel or church and is then followed by a brief prayer and cremation at the crematorium. When a person is buried, the gravestone is likely to be less ornate than that used by Catholics.

Death may be a sad separation for friends and relations, but it is not regarded as the end of that person. It is believed that the removal of the physical body makes it possible for someone to have a much deeper spiritual relationship with Christ. Protestants often speak of death as 'going home'.

1 Were you baptised as a baby (this is also called Christening)? If so, ask your parents *why* they had you baptised.
2 Explain the symbolic meaning of baptism by immersion (going completely under the water).
3 There are two ways of looking at the Christian community. Either Christianity is something shared by many people in society, although not all choose to attend church regularly. Or else, Christianity is restricted to those who are committed and active members of a worshipping community. Which of these views of Christianity do you prefer? Why?
4 Describe in your own words what is meant by a 'born again Christian'.
5 Imagine that you are about to be married. You have to choose between a ceremony in a Registry Office and a wedding in church. What things will you and your partner think about in making your choice?
6 Explain why a registrar is present at some church weddings, in addition to the minister, and what he or she is there to do.
7 Why do you think Christians sometimes refer to death as 'going home'? (What do they regard as the home where they really belong, and who do they think will be with them there?)

# FESTIVALS

The Church of England observes the main festivals of the Catholic tradition, as well as some of the Saints' Days. At the other extreme, a few of the smaller Protestant denominations do not observe any of these festivals, but believe that one day should be treated just like any other. Most Protestant Churches, however, celebrate three festivals during the year. These are:

A nativity play forms part of this Christmas service. The map reminds Christians that Jesus' birth in Bethlehem has importance for the whole world.

(a) What else can you see that shows that this is a Christmas celebration?
(b) What do you think these children are feeling as they play their part in the service?

## Christmas

As in the other branches of the Christian Church, the date chosen for the celebration of the birth of Christ is 25 December. It is a joyful time of feasting and carol-singing. Christmas presents are given, because Christians believe that Jesus was the greatest gift to the world. The poor are helped at this time in particular, so that they too can share in the celebration, and because Jesus was concerned for the poor.

## Easter

This is the celebration of the resurrection of Christ. Easter eggs and flowers represent new life; and churches may be decorated for this season. It is a time when most Christians want to receive Holy Communion.

## Pentecost (or Whitsun)

This festival marks the giving of the Holy Spirit to the disciples, fifty days after Easter. It is seen as the birthday of the Church, since it was only after the first Christian Pentecost that the disciples went out to preach and to establish their new religion. This festival is particularly important for the Pentecostal Churches, which are named after it. These Churches believe that Christians can still feel the power and excitement of the Holy Spirit, as the disciples did at the first Pentecost.

Some Protestant Churches have other events throughout the year. In North America in the nineteenth century there sprang up a tradition of having camp meetings. Large numbers of Christians would go away together and pitch camp in a remote spot. There they would have a time of prayer and Bible study and hear a variety of preachers. Many churches today organise summer camps along similar lines. They combine a family holiday with a programme of religious study and worship.

1 How do we usually celebrate important events? List the things you would expect to find in most celebrations, not just religious ones.
2 Design a card which expresses the religious message of Christmas.
3 Why is Easter the most important of all Christian festivals?
4 How is Easter celebrated by many people who would not claim to be Christian?
5 Read how the first Pentecost started (Acts 2:1–4). Then read the result of Peter's preaching in Acts 2:37–42. (For 'speaking in tongues' see p. 66.)
6 John Wesley, founder of the Methodist Church, often preached in the open air among the people. This tradition is continued today among many Protestant Churches.

# SPECIAL OFFER TO EVERYONE IN SWANLEY

* IMPROVED QUALITY OF LIFE...
* GREATER HAPPINESS...
* BETTER HEALTH...
* PEACE OF MIND...

This is the front cover of a leaflet advertising a Christian campaign. Inside it says: 'International Christian speaker Bob Gordon and his team will be here to help you to find that all these good good things are possible.'

Protestant Churches may arrange special opportunities to preach to those who are outside the Church community. Sometimes these events are called crusades. Well-known preachers — like Billy Graham — attract very large crowds. Crusades like this are generally organised by several churches working together; and people who have been attracted to the crusade are helped to become members of their local churches.

(a) Why do you think some preachers choose this approach?
(b) What problems might they encounter in doing this?
(c) Have you ever heard someone speaking about either religion or politics on a street corner? How did you feel about being appealed to in this way?

# CHECK YOUR READING ON THE PROTESTANT CHURCHES

1 In which century did the Reformation take place?
2 Who wrote the '95 Theses' in 1517?
3 In which city did John Calvin put his ideas into practice?
4 What word, meaning 'elder', has given its name to a denomination?
5 Which king first made himself head of the Church of England?
6 Give another name for the Church of England.
7 What can we call the Churches which broke away from the Church of England?
8 Which state in the USA is named after an early Quaker?
9 Which Church was founded by John Wesley?
10 Who started the Salvation Army?
11 What is likely to be the most dominant piece of furniture in a Protestant chapel?
12 What does the Salvation Army call its places of worship?
13 What is 'extempore' prayer?
14 To what do Protestants turn to find out what they ought to believe?
15 When might a Christian be described as 'born again'?
16 In which Churches are you likely to hear 'speaking in tongues'?
17 What is special about Quaker worship?
18 Which are the two main sacraments in Protestant Churches?
19 Name two denominations which have no sacraments.
20 Name a Church which does not practise infant baptism, but only 'believers' baptism'.
21 Give another name for the service of Holy Communion in Protestant Churches.
22 What does this service commemorate?
23 Which two symbols are used at Holy Communion?
24 What is the most important Christian festival?
25 What does the festival of Pentecost commemorate?

# Some Other Names

In Part 3, we saw some of the features of Protestantism, and a few of the major Protestant Churches were named by way of example. It would have been impossible to describe all the many Protestant Churches, for there are hundreds of them. Once the first Protestants broke away from the central authority of the Roman Catholic Church, there was nothing to stop more and more of them from setting up on their own.

In this section we are going to look at four Churches which began in nineteenth-century North America and which have now become established worldwide. In some ways they are similar to the Protestant Churches. They put great emphasis on the Bible (both Old and New Testaments) and on salvation through Jesus Christ. Their understanding of the Bible tends to be very literal — taking it at its face value; and their beliefs are based on their own interpretation of the Bible. Each Church firmly believes that it has the truth from God, and puts a lot of effort into spreading its message to others. Three of them accept the sacraments of baptism and Holy Communion, practising believers' baptism by full immersion. (Christian Scientists, like the Society of Friends, do not celebrate the sacraments.)

Despite the similarities, these Churches are not dealt with in Part 3 because there are also significant differences in beliefs and practices. The Churches of the three main branches of Christianity see them as outsiders; and both Mormons and Jehovah's Witnesses dissociate themselves from the other Churches, seeing themselves as the only true Christians. It is the distinctive features of these Churches which we shall concentrate on here.

## THE CHURCH OF JESUS CHRIST OF LATTER-DAY SAINTS

Members of this Church are commonly called Mormons. It is now over 150 years old and has a membership of six million.

Joseph Smith, its founder, was born in 1805 and lived in Upper State New York. He was troubled by the competition between the different denominations and did not know which one he should join. Then,

Joseph Smith

77

at the age of fourteen, he started to have visions and said that God the Father and Jesus Christ his Son had told him that all the Churches were in error and that he should restore the true Gospel. Mormons believe that the angel Moroni appeared to him and showed him where to find gold plates, inscribed in ancient languages which, by a miracle, Joseph Smith was able to translate. This became *The Book of Mormon*. In this, the Indian tribes of America were said to be one of the lost tribes of Israel spoken of in the Bible. It said that Jesus Christ himself had visited the Western World, and that the New Jerusalem was to be founded in America. This book, along with the Bible, is regarded by the Mormons as the Word of God. Fired with this vision, Joseph Smith founded his new Church in 1830. From New York, his followers moved on to Ohio and then to Illinois. They met violent opposition, and Joseph Smith was murdered in 1844.

The leadership of the Latter-day Saints passed to Brigham Young. He was a powerful and controversial person. Like some early figures in the Old Testament, he took more than one wife (seventeen in all, of whom nine survived him). This was seen as a scandal by those outside the new Church. Under Young, the Mormons came to the state of Utah. There, based on Salt Lake City, which is still their headquarters, they founded their New Israel in the desert. The Mormon practice of polygamy (marrying more than one wife) was officially discontinued in 1890 when Utah became one of the United States.

A person becomes a member of this Church by baptism and the laying on of hands. Baptism is done by immersion, usually at the age of eight. At this age, young people are considered old enough to make up their own minds about their belief and to feel sorry for their sins, for which they are now held responsible. They believe that only those who have been baptised into the Church of Jesus Christ of Latter-day Saints can enter Heaven. So the Church helps believers to trace their ancestry, so that baptism can be performed on behalf of those who have already died without becoming members.

Another distinctive practice is called Celestial Marriage, where a Mormon husband and wife can choose to have their marriage sealed in heaven. They believe that, in heaven, those who have been married in this way continue as husband and wife and have their families with them. Mormons believe that every person has a spirit which existed with God before he or she was actually born on Earth. Life on Earth is therefore seen as one episode within a continuing spiritual life.

Mormons take their religion very seriously, and live in a healthy and disciplined way. They are not allowed to take drugs; so they do not smoke or drink alcohol (for their Communion sacrament services they use bread and water). Tea and coffee are also banned because they are a

Celestial Marriages are conducted in special 'temples' like this one — the Jordan River Temple in Utah. Ordinary services take place in 'chapels'.

mild form of drug. They argue that these things pollute the body so that it is not fit for God's work.

Mormons give ten per cent of their income to the Church, and on the first Sunday in each month they make a 'fast offering'. This means that they go without their main meal on that day, and contribute the money saved to help those who are poor.

There are no paid ministers, but many people share in the preaching, teaching and social work of the Church. At the age of twelve a boy can be ordained as a deacon, at fourteen as a teacher, and at sixteen as a priest. He may become an elder from the age of eighteen — which is an office within the priesthood. Young men are expected to spend two years working for the Church before they marry or settle down in a career. At any one time there are about twenty-five thousand of these Mormon missionaries throughout the world. They are concerned to promote family life, and to provide educational, health and welfare programmes for members of the Church.

---

1 (a) Joseph Smith was only just over fourteen when he first claimed to have had a vision of God, and only nineteen when he set up a new Church. Can you name any other people, not necessarily religious, who have achieved great things while still young?
(b) Joseph Smith made a big impact in a short life. How old was he when he was killed?
(c) Discuss the advantages and disadvantages that young people may have in starting some new enterprise.
(d) Do you think that the Church is wise to let such young men become religious leaders? Give your reasons.
2 (a) Give some reasons why people drink alcohol or coffee, and smoke tobacco.
(b) What drugs do these contain?
(c) What benefits are there in the Mormon way of life which forbids the use of such drugs?

---

# SEVENTH-DAY ADVENTISTS

Christians have always believed in the glorious Second Coming (or Advent) of Christ at the end of time. It is spoken of in the New Testament. In the early days of Christianity this was expected to happen quite soon, but as time passed it became thought of as a long way in the future. Some Christians may think of it as an idea which expresses the final rule of Christ over everything, rather than as a literal event to be expected.

In the nineteenth century, an American, William Miller, predicted that the Second Advent of Christ would come some time between March 1843 and March 1844. Then, when this date had passed, 22 October 1844 was suggested and the arrival of Christ was eagerly awaited. After that date, some, including Miller himself, admitted that they had made a mistake. This was called 'The Great Disappointment'.

Adventism was taken up by others, including Mrs Ellen G. White. She is regarded as a prophet i.e. Adventists believe that God spoke through her. They still follow her writings, but do not consider them to be Holy Scripture like the Bible.

She claimed to have many visions, as a result of which she taught that Christ had come in 1844, but not to Earth. Instead, he had entered the most holy place of the temple in Heaven. She believed that Christ would visibly come to Earth, and that this would happen soon; but Seventh-day Adventists make no attempt to predict the exact date.

The Adventists who followed Mrs White's interpretation of the Bible became known as Seventh-day Adventists, because she taught that Saturday, and not Sunday, should be kept as the Sabbath (the holy day of rest and worship) — as commanded in the Old Testament.

Adventists do not practise infant baptism,

A Seventh-day Adventist Church in St Albans, Hertfordshire. The Adventists work in 200 countries and the Church is expanding rapidly. The headquarters of the Trans-European Division is in St Albans.

Their logo shows a cross and three flying angels. Can you suggest reasons why?

but insist that each candidate for membership in the church be instructed in their beliefs before being baptised. They give a tithe (that is, ten per cent of their income) to the work of the Church, and agree to abstain from drugs, including alcohol and tobacco. They try to follow a healthy diet and are not allowed 'unclean' foods which, following the Old Testament laws, include pig meat and some sea foods, as well as tea and coffee.

They celebrate the Lord's Supper (Holy Communion), usually once every three months, and every Church member is encouraged to attend. This service includes footwashing, because Jesus did this at the Last Supper as well as sharing the bread and wine. It is taken as a sign of humility, and expresses the washing away of sins that have been committed since the last celebration. For the Communion, they use unleavened bread and non-alcoholic grape juice.

Adventists emphasise the Second Coming of Christ, and therefore speak out (prophesy) about what is to happen. They broadcast internationally through the Adventist World Radio network. In Europe their radio station is called The Voice of Hope. There is an International Bible Correspondence School called The Voice of Prophecy, and in the United States there is a telecast called Faith for Today. Like many of the other smaller denominations, great emphasis is placed on missionary work, and the Seventh-day Adventists have many publishing houses producing books and magazines to promote their beliefs. The total baptised membership today of this Church is five million.

1 Explain why the name Seventh-day Adventist is used.
2 How does the Adventist attitude to the writings of Mrs White differ from the Mormon attitude to the *Book of Mormon*?
3 Before sharing in the Lord's Supper, Adventists wash one another's feet, women and men sitting separately.
(a) What is the origin of this ceremony? (see John 13:1–15)
(b) Explain the meaning this has for Adventists.
4 (a) Do you ever read your 'Stars'? If so, do you take them seriously?
(b) How else do people predict the future?
(c) How do you react to *either* prophecies about the end of the world, *or* predictions based on the Bible?

# JEHOVAH'S WITNESSES

Charles Taze Russell (1852–1916) started Bible classes in Pittsburgh, Pennsylvania, having become dissatisfied with all existing forms of the Christian religion. He founded Zion's Watchtower Society, published interpretations of the Bible, and spent much of his time preaching and selling religious pamphlets (usually called 'tracts').

Since 1931, those who follow his tradition of Bible Study have been known as 'Jehovah's Witnesses'. They call God by the name used for him in some English translations of the Old Testament — Jehovah. They are 'Witnesses' because they believe they have a duty to share their beliefs with others, as the early Christians did. There are now more than three million Jehovah's Witnesses worldwide, about three quarters of them outside the United States.

Like Adventists, they look for the Second Coming of Christ. Because of people's sin, Witnesses expect that the world will soon come to an end. Originally, it was believed that 1914 would be the year in which the Archangel Gabriel would blow his trumpet and Christ return to Earth to announce the establishment of his Kingdom. Jehovah's Witnesses now claim that Christ's Kingdom was set up in heaven in 1914, that we are living in the last days, and that evil will soon be destroyed and God will rule over a New Earth.

There are two classes of people, according to Jehovah's Witnesses. One hundred and forty-four thousand of those who have been faithful form what is called the 'anointed class'. They are destined to rule with Christ. This number was completed by 1935, and all the other Witnesses form the second class (or 'great crowd') and are to enjoy life in a Paradise on Earth, after the destruction of evil.

They take the words of the Bible literally, and because of this they refuse to have blood transfusions. The Old Testament forbids the eating of blood in meat, and Witnesses argue that, if it is wrong to take blood into the body through the mouth, it must also be wrong to take it directly into the veins. Sometimes legal action is taken to overrule the wishes of parents who are Jehovah's Witnesses and whose children are in danger of death if they do not receive blood.

Witnesses do not celebrate Christmas or Easter, because there is no mention of these festivals in the Bible. The only thing Jesus commanded to be done in memory of his death was Holy Communion, so this service is held once a year.

Witnesses are organised locally in a 'congregation' which meets in a 'Kingdom Hall'. The organisation and worship is led by 'elders' and 'servants'. They do not have paid ministers, and each member is required to act as a missionary, distributing copies of their magazines (one of which is called *Watchtower*) to promote their beliefs.

Some people are attracted to the

Jehovah's Witnesses because of their simple and literal interpretation of the Bible, the unquestioned authority this has for them, and the very positive view it gives of the future. Witnesses do not believe that a God of love would allow everlasting torment in Hell. They think the dead will be raised to life when Christ comes at the Day of Judgement, and will be given the chance to live on the newly formed Earth. People who continue to reject Christ will then be destroyed, along with everything that is evil. They tend to point to natural disasters and troubles in the world as signs that the destruction promised by God is soon to arrive.

Jehovah's Witnesses are assured that they are the only true Christians and they are critical of all other forms of organised religion, believing other denominations to be under the control of the Devil.

1 Why do you think this young Church has been able to grow to more than three million? Give as many reasons as you can.
2 Can you see any similarity between the Seventh-day Adventists insisting on Saturday as the holy day and the Jehovah's Witnesses rejecting blood transfusions? Think of the reason each Church gives.
3 'Real Christians can give gifts and have good times together throughout the year. (Luke 6:38) Parents do not have to wait for birthdays or for Christmas, but they can bring gifts to their children at various times during the year. This makes for many happy occasions instead of one or two.' (*The Truth that leads to Eternal Life*, Watch Tower Bible and Tract Society, p. 150.)
(a) What disadvantages would there be for Jehovah's Witnesses living in countries where Christmas is a popular time of celebration?
(b) Looking at the alternatives in the quotation, which would you prefer?

# THE CHURCH OF CHRIST, SCIENTIST (CHRISTIAN SCIENCE)

This Church was founded in Boston, Massachusetts in 1879 by Mary Baker Eddy. Some years before this she had a remarkable recovery from a fall, and believed that she had experienced God's healing power. She was so impressed with this that she studied the accounts of healing among the early Christians, and wrote a book called *Science and Health with Key to the Scriptures*.

This book, along with the Bible, is the basis of Christian Science belief. In it she argued that God had made everything good, and formed people in his own image. Suffering, death and evil are therefore 'illusion', because they are not made by a loving God. They may *seem* very real, but only in the way that events in a dream may seem real to a dreamer. Christian Scientists believe that once a person realises that he or she is at one with God, and the physical world of matter is not the solid reality it appears to be, then God comes into that person's life in healing and wholeness.

Heaven and hell are not believed to be places to which the good or wicked will be sent after death, but are states of mind that a person can experience. A person who does wrong will create his or her own hell, and the person who does good, finds heaven.

Christian Science is concerned with both physical healing of disease, and the promotion of a healthy and spiritual attitude to life. Members of the Church are meant to pray, to study their beliefs a little each day, and to be merciful, just and pure in their lives.

There are nearly three thousand Christian Science churches, about three quarters of which are in the United States. There are no ministers, but there are 'practitioners' who devote their time to the healing

Every Christian Science church has a reading room where people can go to study and pray. They have many publications, probably the best-known of which is the newspaper, *The Christian Science Monitor*.

ministry. Worship consists of hymns, prayers and readings from the Bible and from *Science and Health*. The 'sermon' is not something which a minister preaches, but consists of readings from these books. The members themselves elect those who are to lead the services. They do not celebrate the sacraments, although they believe that the ideas expressed in baptism and Holy Communion are important.

For most Christians, suffering and death are real, and they see Christ's death on the cross as helping them to face and overcome them. Christian Science is distinctive in saying that we don't see things now as they really are, and that suffering and evil are an 'illusion' that can be destroyed through God's power. People are not limited to the world of matter, but are spiritual beings, like God himself.

1  Some people describe things as 'heavenly' or talk about 'hell on earth'. What do people mean by talking about experiencing heaven or hell here and now?
2  Do you think there is any truth in saying that illness is 'all in the mind'? Can you think of any time when you have either made yourself feel worse or better by thinking about your illness in a particular way?

83

# The Worldwide Church

## THE ECUMENICAL MOVEMENT

In the New Testament, the variety within the Christian community is described in terms of the many parts of a single body. It was never imagined that all Christians would be exactly the same as one another. What mattered was that they should accept one another and be able to work together.

We have seen how different groups of Christians have separated from one another in order to believe and worship in their own particular way. This was often as a protest against the beliefs and attitudes of other Christians. In the past, these divisions have led to savage persecution and hostility between one part of the Christian community and another.

Many Christians felt that this was against the will of Christ, who had prayed that all his disciples should be one. Missionaries in particular saw that if the Christian message was to be preached with conviction, it was important that the Churches should be seen to work together and not against one another. So from the end of the eighteenth century, Christian missionary societies were formed by several Churches together. The same was true of Bible societies — Churches wanted to combine their resources for publishing and distributing the Scriptures. Another movement supported by different denominations was the Young Men's Christian Association, which still flourishes all over the world with hostels for men and now also for women (through the YWCA, founded later).

This was the beginning of the Ecumenical Movement. The word *ecumenical* comes from a Greek word meaning 'the whole inhabited world'. The Ecumenical Movement therefore stands for the ways in which Christians of different denominations have come together.

## THE WORLD COUNCIL OF CHURCHES

The main organisation today for bringing together Christians of different denominations is the World Council of Churches. It was started in 1948 and now has a membership of more than three hundred Churches. These include the Orthodox Churches. The Roman Catholic Church is not a member, but shares in some of the work of the Council, and sends observers to its main meetings. The work of the WCC is divided into three programmes:

(i) *Faith and witness*
This programme studies the beliefs which have divided Christians in the past, helps Churches to work together in missionary work, and seeks to build bridges between Christians and those of other faiths.

(ii) *Justice and service*
This programme is concerned with world development, with aid for the Third World, with refugees and with the problems of racial oppression.

(iii) *Education and renewal*
This programme is concerned with education and training. It helps local Christian groups, and is particularly concerned with the place of women and young people in the churches.

The second Assembly of the World Council of Churches, at Evanston, Illinois, USA. Christians came together from all over the world to discuss the theme: 'Christ, the hope of the world'. Between 1948 and 1983 there were six such assemblies, held in different parts of the world.

Notice the WCC emblem. The ship represents the Church afloat on the sea of the world. What does the Greek word surrounding it mean?

Recently the WCC arranged for a hundred religious scholars, from most denominations, to consider the teaching of their Churches on baptism, Holy Communion and the ministry. They met in Lima in Peru, and in 1982 they produced the *Lima Document* in which they reached considerable agreement.

**The British Council of Churches**, formed in 1942, is associated with the World Council of Churches, and its activities in Britain are similar to those of the World Council. Within it there are many local Councils of Churches, which help Christians of different denominations to work together in their own areas. Perhaps the best known of its organisations is Christian Aid. Each year, Christian Aid Week brings Christians from the different Churches together in their common concern to raise money for the Third World.

# UNITED CHURCHES

We have seen that ecumenical work is far more than bringing different Churches together to form single denominations, but this too has happened in recent years:

**1947 The Church of South India** was formed by the combination of the Anglican, Methodist and the South India United Church (which had combined the Presbyterian and Congregational Churches).
**1970 The United Church of North India** was formed from these same denominations, but with the Baptists as well
**1972 The United Reformed Church** came into being as a result of the joining of the Congregational Church in England and Wales with the Presbyterian Church in England.

As one of its many projects throughout the world, Christian Aid supports a programme to immunise children in Bangladesh. Salma, who is giving the injection, has been trained to assist the doctors and nurses —because there are not enough of them.

(a) What diseases have you been immunised against?
(b) What other help do you think someone like Salma could give, without being fully qualified as a nurse?

The meeting in Rome of Pope Paul VI and Michael Ramsey, the Archbishop of Canterbury. This historic event in 1966 was the first time the leaders of the Roman Catholic Church and the Anglican Church had met since the Reformation. It marked the beginning of better relationships between these two Churches. Since then there have been joint discussions on important issues which divide them, such as their understanding of Holy Communion and the priesthood.

Other attempts at drawing Churches together in this way have been less successful. For some years there was discussion about a combined future for the Anglican and Methodist Churches, but in 1969 and again in 1972 proposals for this were rejected by the Anglican side. Since then there has been a wider attempt to get Churches to agree not to do anything apart which they could do together.

# UNITED COMMUNITIES

There are also religious communities which work to overcome the divisions between denominations. Two of these are:

### Corrymeela
Northern Ireland has seen much bitterness between Catholics and Protestants. At Corrymeela (a name which means 'Hill of Harmony'), a community works to bring Catholics and Protestants together so that they can understand one another better. Christians at Corrymeela believe that the deep divisions in Northern Ireland can only be bridged if people meet one another and form personal ties of friendship. Corrymeela also provides a place of peace and rest for those who are affected by the violence in Northern Ireland.

### Taizé
This community of monks was founded by Roger Schutz in order to help those who were escaping from Nazi-controlled France during the Second World War. Taizé has become an ecumenical community which attracts people from all over the world. Monks at Taizé come from all three branches of the Church — Protestant, Catholic and Orthodox. Much of the

A gathering of young people at Taizé. Choose four words which you think describe the mood of the people in the photograph.

worship is shared across the divisions between denominations, although when it comes to receiving Communion there are separate parts of the same church building for Catholics and Protestants.

Taizé has been concerned to help the young people of the world come together and listen to one another. In particular it encourages those of the northern hemisphere to understand the natural spirit of festivity which can be found among the people of the poorer south.

So Taizé is an ecumenical community in both senses of that word — it draws together the different Christian groups, and it also has a concern for the whole world.

In 1974 the Council of Youth opened at Taizé, attracting young people from every continent to join in a time of thought and action in order to understand the challenge of being Christian in the world today. Since then there have been international gatherings of young people, with many thousands taking part, in different European cities and also in Madras, India.

Brothers from the Taizé community work in many places alongside the very poor. They seek to create a Church which is without wealth or political power, and which is ready to share with all, so that it can be a place where all people can come together. Many of those who go to Taizé think of themselves as belonging to the worldwide Church first of all, and only after that do they think about their particular denomination. This ecumenical vision helps them to work happily alongside those whose ways of expressing the Christian faith may differ from their own.

1 Look up 1 Corinthians 12:12 to the end. What attitude do you think St Paul was trying to promote among the Christians of Corinth?
2 Sometimes people find it very difficult to accept those whose religious views differ from their own. Why do you think religious debates can stir up such strong feelings?
3 Copy out the words of John 17:11b.
4 Design a badge for an ecumenical community which is concerned with people throughout the world. (The one for the World Council of Churches is shown in the photograph on p. 85.)
5 Make a note of when the World Council of Churches was founded, of how many denominations belong to it, and of one important Church which is not a member.
6 (a) Give an example of the World Council of Churches' work to bring together different Christian Churches.
(b) Give an example of the World Council of Churches' concern to help the whole world (not just Christians).

# Word List

**absolution** the assurance, given by a priest after a person's confession, that his or her sins are forgiven

**Advent** 'arrival' — season of preparation for Christmas; Second Advent — expected return of Christ to Earth

**Adventists** those whose beliefs emphasise the Second Coming of Christ

**altar** a place where sacrifice takes place: used (particularly by Catholics) for the table at which the Communion Service is celebrated

**Anglican** another name for the Church of England and associated Churches

**annulment** the legal process in the Catholic Church which declares that a marriage is not valid and may therefore be set aside

**Apostle/apostolic** one who is 'sent out' — used of the earliest followers of Jesus; adj. of Apostle(s)

**baptism** the sacrament by which a person becomes a member of the Church, used by most denominations, involving immersion in or splashing with water

**baptistery** a tank of water used for baptism by immersion; may also be used for the part of a church building which contains a font

**bishop** a church leader who has responsibility for the churches of an area called a diocese

**cardinal** a senior member of the Catholic Church (usually a bishop) who can vote in the election of a new pope

**cassock** long robe worn by some priests and ministers

**cathedral** the main church of a diocese, used as the base for the work of its bishop

**catholic** 'worldwide' — used especially of the churches under the authority of the Bishop of Rome (the Roman Catholic Church)

**celestial** 'heavenly' — used of the 'sealing' of Mormon marriages

**chapel** a place of worship, especially one belonging to the Free Churches; also used of those parts of a large church or cathedral which have their own altars (side chapel; Lady Chapel, when dedicated to the Virgin Mary)

**Charismatic** a Christian who feels empowered by the 'gifts' of the Holy Spirit; adj. used of churches, especially Pentecostal

**chrismation** anointing with oil, performed after baptism in the Orthodox Churches

**Christ** 'the anointed one' — Jewish idea of the Saviour, used of Jesus

**Christmas** festival to celebrate the birth of Christ

**Church/church** a group of Christians; the building where they meet for worship

**confession** a statement of sorrow for sins that have been committed, and the request for forgiveness, made by an individual privately to God, or through a priest; a general confession may be made by a whole group of Christians together

**confirmation** a service in the Catholic Church and some Protestant Churches during which a person agrees to become a full member of the Church, and is 'made firm' in this by the Holy Spirit, through the 'laying on of hands' by a bishop

**congregation** a group of Christians gathered together (usually for worship and in a church building)

**consecrated** 'made holy' — used especially of the bread and wine in the Communion service

**conversion/convert** 'to turn' — used of a person's acceptance of a particular religion

**covenant** an agreement; used of the relationship between God and his people

**creed** a statement of beliefs

**cremation** the burning of a corpse as an alternative to burial

**crucifix** the image of Jesus on the cross

**deacon** 'servant' — a person who assists the priest

**dedicate** to offer something to God for a special purpose (used of buildings and also of children)

**denomination** 'name' — used of different Christian groups

**devotion** act of worship

**diocese** area of churches ruled by a bishop

**disciple** a follower; used especially of the earliest followers of Jesus

**doctrine** teachings (of the Church)

**Easter** Christian festival celebrating the resurrection of Christ

**ecumenical** 'of the whole inhabited world' — used of the whole Church, and of the movement to bring denominations together

**Epiphany** 'showing forth' — used of the festival held on 6 January to celebrate the showing forth of Jesus to the world

**eternal** everlasting

**Eucharist** 'giving thanks' — used of the Communion Service

**excommunicate** to expel from the Church

**extempore** used of prayers offered in a person's own words without preparation

**fasting** going without food as part of spiritual discipline

**font** container of water for baptism

**friar** a person who belongs to one of the orders of friars (Dominican or Franciscan) and who is therefore committed to a life of simplicity and poverty, working at preaching, teaching and caring for those in need

**Good Friday** the Friday before Easter; the day of Jesus' death

**Gospel** the 'good news' of Jesus; also used of readings from the four Gospels in the New Testament

**grace** prayer of thanksgiving at mealtime

**hermit** one who lives alone in an isolated place

**holy** chosen and 'set aside' for a religious purpose

**Holy Communion** service where bread and wine are consecrated, following the example of Jesus at the Last Supper

**Holy Spirit** one of the three Persons of the Trinity; God working through and influencing people

**holy water** water that has been blessed

**Holy Week** the name given by the Church to the week leading up to Easter Day

**icon** special painting of Jesus or one of the saints, used mainly in Orthodox worship

**iconostasis** icon-screen across the front of an Orthodox church

**idolatry** worshipping something other than God

**incense** spice burned during worship

**infallible** the Roman Catholic teaching that the pope cannot be wrong when speaking with the full authority of his position on certain matters of belief and morality

**Julian calendar** The Julian and Gregorian calendars (named after Roman emperors) are ways of dividing up the year.

**justified** being 'set right' – used of a person's relationship with God

**Last Supper** the last meal Jesus ate with his disciples before his death

**lay/laity** members of a church who are not ordained

**laying on of hands** the ritual of placing both hands on a person's head

**lectern** a stand for holding the Bible when it is read out in church

**Liturgy** Orthodox term for the Communion Service

**Lost Tribes** There were originally twelve tribes of Israel. Ten of these, from the northern part of Israel, were disbanded or 'lost' after the political disturbances at the end of the eighth century BCE. What happened to them is generally unknown, but Mormons believe that one of them went to America

**martyr** 'witness' — one who dies for his or her faith

**Mass** Catholic name for the Communion Service

**Maundy Thursday** the Thursday before Easter; named after Jesus' 'command' (Latin *mandatum*) that the disciples should love one another

**minister** used especially in the Free Churches of the person who is chosen to lead the worship of a church

**missionary** a person who is 'sent out' to preach his or her faith and to convert others

**mitre** pointed hat worn by a bishop, shaped to represent the flames of Pentecost

**monk/monastery** a man who takes vows of poverty, chastity and obedience, and lives with others in a monastery

**mystery** something which human minds are unable to understand; **Mystery** – Orthodox name for a sacrament

**nun** a woman who takes vows of poverty, chastity and obedience, and lives with others in a convent

**offertory** the point in a Communion Service when bread and wine (and money) are taken to the altar or Communion table

**ordain/ordination** the sacrament by which a person is made a priest or deacon

**orthodox** 'right belief' — used especially of the Eastern Orthodox Churches

**pacifist** one who refuses to use violence to support any cause

**parish** where there is an official or 'established' church in a country (e.g. the Anglican Church in England), the whole of that country is divided up into areas called parishes, each of which is served by a local church

**paschal** 'of Passover'; since Jesus died at Passover, this describes things to do with Easter

**patriarch** 'great father' — title of the leaders of the Orthodox Churches

**penance** 'punishment' — the recommended discipline following confession

**Pentecost** the Jewish festival in which the disciples are said to have been first filled with the Holy Spirit; it therefore became a Christian festival, also called Whitsun

**Pentecostal** a denomination which emphasises the Gifts of the Spirit at Pentecost

**pilgrim** one who makes a journey for a religious purpose

**polygamy** having more than one wife

**pope** the title given to the Bishop of Rome; meaning 'father', it was once used for all bishops, and is still used of the head of the Coptic Church in Egypt

**praying** speaking and listening to God

**priest** one ordained to act as an agent and representative between people and God

**prophecy** that which is spoken out in the name of God, used especially of warnings about the future

**Protestant** n. 'one who protests' adj. 'of the protesters' — used particularly of the reforms started in the sixteenth century, and the branch of the Church which developed from these

**Puritan** used especially in the seventeenth century of those who wanted to 'purify' the Church of England of Catholic practices

**Reformation** period in the sixteenth century when the Protestant reformers broke away from the Roman Catholic Church

**relics** sacred objects associated with Jesus or one of the saints; venerated especially in the Middle Ages

**resurrection** 'raising up' — used especially of Jesus after his death

**revelation** that which is revealed/made known by God

**ritual** a religious ceremony

**Sabbath** seventh day of the week (Saturday); a day of rest in the Jewish religion

**sacrament** a ritual through which God is believed to work (Catholics accept seven sacraments, most Protestants only two. In the Orthodox tradition, the sacraments are referred to as 'Mysteries'.)

**sacrifice** something of value which is offered up (often to be killed) in the course of an act of worship

**saint** a holy person — applies to all Christians, but some especially known for

their holiness are officially called 'Saints'

**saint's day** day set aside each year in honour of a particular saint, often the day of his or her death

**salvation** 'saving' of the soul

**scriptures** 'writings' — a holy book

**sermon** talk given by a priest or minister, preached in the course of a service

**sin** that which is against God's will

**speaking in tongues** praising God in strange languages which Christians believe are given them by the Holy Spirit

**spiritual** 'of the spirit' — as opposed to (physical/material) things which can be seen and touched

**symbol** that which points beyond itself to a deeper meaning

**tabernacle** box containing consecrated bread

**tithe** a 'tenth' of income, given to the Church

**transubstantiation** the Catholic doctrine that the substance of the bread and wine are changed into the Body and Blood of Christ in the Communion Service

**Trinity** the Christian teaching that God exists as three Persons: Father, Son and Holy Spirit, often referred to as the Holy Trinity

**Unction** traditional name for the Sacrament of the Sick in the Catholic Church, involving anointing with oil

**unleavened** (of bread) made without yeast

**venerate** to show respect but not worship (used especially of icons in the Orthodox tradition)

**vestments** special clothes worn by clergy during religious services

**vision** something seen in a trance

**Zion** a name for Jerusalem, which was built on Mount Zion

# Useful Addresses

The National Society's R.E. Centre
23 Kensington Square
London W8 5HN
01–937 4241
(reference library for world religions; book lists and leaflets)

Education Consultant
Baptist Union of Great Britain
4 Southampton Row
London WC1B 4AB
01–405 9803

British Council of Churches
Inter-Church House
35–41 Lower Marsh
London SE1 7RL
01–620 4444

Westminster Diocesan Education Service
33 Wilfred Street
London SW1E 6PS
01–834 7987
(Roman Catholic)

Catholic Information Office
Avante House, 9 Bridge Street
Pinner, Middlesex HA5 3HR

Catholic Truth Society
38–40 Eccleston Square
London SW1V 1PD
01–834 4392

Schools Officer
Board of Education of Church of England
Church House, Dean's Yard
Westminster, London SW1P 3NZ
01–222 9011

Evangelical Alliance
19 Draycott Place
London SW3
01–581 0051

Education Consultant
Free Church Federal Council
27 Tavistock Square
London WC1H 9HH
01–387 8413

The Methodist Church
Division of Education and Youth
2 Chester House, Pages Lane
London N10 1PR
O1–444 9845

The Most Revd Archbishop Athenagoras II
of Thyateira and Great Britain
Church of the Annunciation
5 Craven Hill, London W2
(Greek Orthodox)

His Eminence The Most Revd Metropolitan
Anthony of Sourozh
Cathedral of the Assumption and All Saints
Ennismore Gardens
London SW7
(Russian Orthodox)

General Secretary
Quaker Education Department
Friends House
Euston Road
London NW1 2BJ
01–387 3601

Salvation Army
101 Queen Victoria Street
London EC4P 4EP
01–236 5222

United Reformed Church House
86 Tavistock Place
London WC1H 9RT
01–837 7661

# Index